COFFEE OBSESSION

COFFEE OBSESSION

Anette Moldvaer

LONDON, NEW YORK,
MUNICH, MELBOURNE, DELHI

DK UK
Project Editor Martha Burley
Art Editor Kathryn Wilding
Design Assistant Kate Fenton
Managing Editor Dawn Henderson
Managing Art Editor Christine Keilty
Senior Jacket Creative Nicola Powling
Senior Cartographic Editor Simon Mumford
Production, Pre-Producer Sarah Isle, Raymond Williams
Production Producer Oliver Jeffreys
Art Director Peter Luff
Category Publisher Peggy Vance

DK INDIA
Project Editor Manasvi Vohra
Senior Art Editor Anchal Kaushal
Editor K. Nungshithoibi Singha
Art Editor Tanya Mehrotra
Assistant Art Editor Pallavi Kapur
Managing Editor Alicia Ingty
Managing Art Editor Navidita Thapa
Pre-Production Manager Sunil Sharma
DTP Designers Anurag Trivedi, Manish Upreti

First published in Great Britain in 2014 by
Dorling Kindersley Limited
80 Strand, London WC2R 0RL

4 6 8 10 9 7 5 3
009 – 192995 – Jul/14

Copyright © 2014
Dorling Kindersley Limited
A Penguin Random House Company

A CIP catalogue record for this book is available
from the British Library.

A NOTE ON THE MAPS: See page 224

ISBN 978-1-4093-5468-0
Colour reproduction by Alta Image
Printed and bound in China

Discover more at **www.dk.com**

CONTENTS

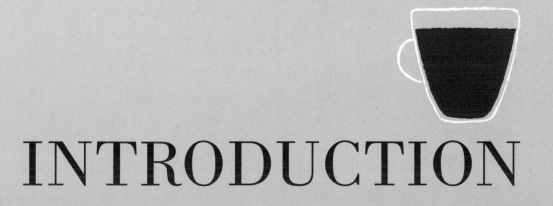

INTRODUCTION

CAFÉ CULTURE

For millions all over the world, sitting in a café with a delicious coffee is one of life's great pleasures. Elevating this experience is the speciality café – where a skilled barista can make you a good-quality coffee, just how you like it.

THE CAFÉ EXPERIENCE

Cafés are at the heart of established traditions that go back centuries – from the café au lait in a Parisian café to the bottomless coffee mug in a Texan diner. More of us frequent cafés than ever before, thanks to coffee's flourishing popularity in China, India, Russia, and Japan. Even though drinking coffee is just a normal part of everyday life for many, it is still a new and exciting experience for countless others.

With this fresh passion for coffee, every day an increasing number of speciality cafés open around the world. Visiting such cafés, where you can experience an array of varieties, roasts, and styles, is no longer just for coffee connoisseurs. For anyone who appreciates the value of quality, sustainability, and care, a speciality coffee house is the perfect place to socialize, explore new flavours, and soak up a unique atmosphere.

COFFEE IS JUST PART OF LIFE FOR MANY, BUT FOR SOME IT IS A NEW AND EXCITING PHENOMENON

THE CAFÉ ETHOS

It is so easy to take coffee's long journey from farm to cup for granted. Not everyone is aware that a coffee bean is the seed of a fruit, or that it needs to be roasted before it can be ground and brewed. An increasing number of cafés treat coffee as the fresh, seasonal product that it is, and promote it as an ingredient and a drink that takes skill to grow and prepare. They highlight and celebrate the vast range of unique flavours out there, helping to reveal the provenance and human story behind the beans.

Thanks to speciality cafés, coffee lovers are becoming aware of the complexities of production, trade, and preparation. The challenges growers face – with low prices and a treacherous commodity market – have spurred an increasing demand for sustainably traded coffees. The concept that "quality costs more" has long been acceptable when it comes to food and wine, and rapidly consumers are realizing that the same rule should apply to coffee.

While the balance between supply, demand, cost, and ecology is one that remains challenging and unpredictable, speciality coffee companies lead with a focus on quality, transparency, and sustainability. With such an increasing cultural shift that focuses on coffee cultivation and preparation, speciality cafés are more important than ever.

THE BARISTA

A barista in a speciality café is akin to a sommelier in the world of wine. He or she is a professional with expert knowledge, capable of advising you on how to prepare coffee in a way that not only gives you a caffeine kick, but also makes it taste interesting, exciting, and, most importantly, good.

THE JOURNEY OF COFFEE

The history of how coffee spread across the world is a story of a world changing. It is a story of religion, slavery, smuggling, love, and community. Although gaps remain, we can trace its journey with the help of both fact and legend.

EARLY DISCOVERIES

Coffee was discovered at least 1,000 years ago. No one knows for sure, but many believe that the origins of Arabica lie in South Sudan and Ethiopia, and that Robusta was born in West Africa.

Even before the seeds were roasted, ground, and brewed to make the coffee we drink today, coffee cherries and leaves were used for their invigorating properties. Travelling herders in Africa mixed coffee seeds with fat and spices to create "energy bars" for the long periods of time spent away from their homes. The coffee leaves and cherry skin were also boiled to create an invigorating, caffeine-rich infusion.

It is thought that coffee was carried to Yemen and Arabia by African slaves. In the 1400s, Sufis drank a tea made from coffee cherries called "quishr" or "Arabian wine" that helped them to stay awake during nightly prayers. The news of its stimulating effects spread, and spaces opened where traders and scholars could drink and interact freely, known as "schools for the wise". Some people worried that quishr was incompatible with religious beliefs, but these early cafés stayed open and increased coffee's popularity. By the 1500s, Arabs had started to roast and grind the cherry beans to create a coffee much like that we enjoy today, which spread to Turkey, Egypt, and North Africa.

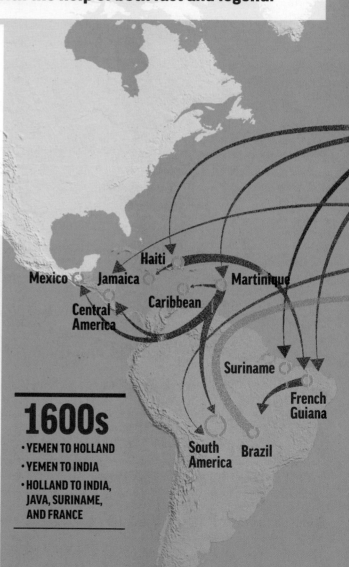

Mexico · Haiti · Jamaica · Martinique · Caribbean · Central America · Suriname · French Guiana · South America · Brazil

1600s
- YEMEN TO HOLLAND
- YEMEN TO INDIA
- HOLLAND TO INDIA, JAVA, SURINAME, AND FRANCE

COLONIAL SPREAD

The first to trade coffee, the Arabs were so protective of their coffee that they boiled the beans so that no one else could cultivate them.

However, in the early 1600s, a Sufi smuggled seeds from Yemen to India and a Dutch trader smuggled seedlings from Yemen and planted them in Amsterdam. By the end of the 17th century, coffee had been planted in the Dutch colonies, particularly throughout Indonesia.

The Caribbean and South American colonies planted coffee in the early 1700s. The Dutch gave seedlings as a gift to the French, who took them to Haiti, Martinique, and French Guiana. The Dutch planted their coffee in Suriname, and the British brought coffee from Haiti to Jamaica.

In 1727, the Portuguese sent a naval officer from Brazil to French Guiana to bring back coffee seeds. Legend has it that he was denied, so seduced the Governor's wife, who smuggled them to him in a bouquet spiked with seedlings.

From South America and the Caribbean, coffee spread to Central America and Mexico. Towards the end of the 1800s, coffee seedlings were returned to colonies in Africa.

Today, coffee production has also spread to new areas of the world, particularly Asia.

Holland

France

Yemen

India

East Africa

Réunion Island

Java

1800s

- **BRAZIL TO EAST AFRICA**
- **RÉUNION TO EAST AFRICA**

1700s

- **FRANCE TO HAITI, MARTINIQUE, FRENCH GUIANA, AND RÉUNION ISLAND**
- **RÉUNION TO CENTRAL AND SOUTH AMERICA**
- **MARTINIQUE TO CARIBBEAN, CENTRAL AND SOUTH AMERICA**
- **HAITI TO JAMAICA**
- **FRENCH GUIANA TO BRAZIL**

WITHIN A FEW HUNDRED YEARS, COFFEE HAD REACHED AROUND THE WORLD, FIRST AS A BEVERAGE, THEN AS A COMMODITY

SPECIES AND VARIETIES

As with grapes for wine and hops for beer, coffee cherries come from a tree that has numerous species and varieties. Although only a few of these spread across the world, new varieties are continually being cultivated.

COFFEA SPECIES

The genus of this flowering tree is called *Coffea*. A modern way of classifying *Coffea* is evolving, as scientists continually discover new species. Nobody knows exactly how many there are, but to date, around 124 species of *Coffea* have been identified – more than double that of just 20 years ago.

Coffea species are found growing wild, mainly in Madagascar and Africa, as well as in the Mascarene Islands, Comoros, Asia, and Australia.

Only the species *C. Arabica* and *C. Canephora* (commonly known as Arabica and Robusta) are widely grown for commercial purposes, representing around 99 per cent of production worldwide. It is believed that *C. Arabica* came from a cross of *C. Canephora* and *C. Eugenioides* that happened around the border of Ethiopia and South Sudan. Some countries also grow small amounts of *C. Liberica* and *C. Excelsa* for local consumption.

ARABICA AND ROBUSTA VARIETIES

There are many cultivated varieties of Arabica. Records of how it spread around the world are incomplete and sometimes conflicting, but of the thousands of native varieties in Ethiopia and South Sudan, only a few were taken out of Africa, first to Yemen, and from there to other countries (see pp10–11).

These trees were referred to as Typica, a generalized name for "ordinary" coffee. Typica trees planted in Java were the genetic starting point for the trees that spread to the rest of the world. Bourbon, another of our earliest known varieties, was a natural mutation of Typica that took place from around the mid-18th to the late 19th century on Bourbon Island, now known as Réunion Island. Today, most varieties are natural or cultivated mutations of these two varieties.

C. Canephora was native to West Africa. From the Belgian Congo, seedlings were also planted in Java. From there it spread across the world, to nearly all of the Arabica-producing countries. There are several varieties of the species, but they are all commonly referred to as simply Robusta. In addition, Arabica and Robusta have been cultivated together to create new varieties.

The look and flavour of coffee is influenced by many forces, such as soil, sun exposure, rainfall patterns, wind patterns, pests, and diseases. Many varieties are genetically similar, but have acquired different regional or local names. This makes it difficult to map accurately the development of Arabica and Robusta, but the family tree (overleaf) shows some of the most commonly grown varieties of these species.

THE COFFEA GENUS

Sun exposure
Most varieties prefer shade or semi-shade. Some are developed to tolerate full sun exposure.

Rainfall patterns
Whether a farm receives frequent showers throughout the year or is in an area with defined wet and dry seasons, rainfall patterns determine flowering times.

Wind patterns
The movement of hot and cold air influences how the coffee cherries mature and taste.

COFFEA
Kingdom: Plantae
Class: Equisetopsida
Subclass: Magnoliidae
Superorder: Asteranae
Order: Gentianales
Family: Rubiaceae
Sub family: Ixoroideae
Tribe: Coffeeae
Genus: Coffea
Main commercial species: Coffea Arabica and Coffea Canephora (commonly known as Robusta)

Cherry clusters
Coffee cherries mature in clusters along the branches.

Coffee flowers
These flowers are sweet-scented, reminiscent of jasmine.

Unripe coffee cherry
Cherries grow to full size as green, hard fruit.

Softened coffee cherry
The fruit slowly changes colour and softens.

Ripe coffee cherry
Most cherries turn red, although varieties exist.

Overripe coffee cherry
Cherries sweeten as they deepen in colour, but turn bad quickly.

Cross-section
Each cherry contains mucilage, parchment, and seeds (see p16).

THE FAMILY TREE

This simplified tree helps to explain the key relationships in the coffee family. As botanists discover new species and varieties with interesting flavours and properties, the family tree continues to grow and develop.

More research is needed before we can show the relationships between all coffee varieties in existence, but this illustration shows four of the species in the Rubiaceae family: Liberica, Robusta, Arabica, and Excelsa. Of these four species, only Arabica and Robusta are commercially grown (see pp12–13). Robusta varieties, largely considered to be of lower quality than Arabicas, are known simply as Robustas.

From the main branch of the Arabica species stem the Heirloom varieties, as well as Typica and Bourbon varieties and their crosses. Robustas are also occasionally crossed with Arabica to create hybrids.

HYBRIDS

Rasuna Catimor + Typica
Arabusta Arabica + Robusta
Devamachy Arabica + Robusta
Hibrido de Timor/TimTim/BorBor Arabica + Robusta
Icatu Bourbon + Robusta + Mundo Novo
Ruiru 11 Rune Sudan + K7 + SL 28 + Catimor
Sarchimor Villa Sarchi + Hibrido de Timor

C.CANEPHORA (ROBUSTA)

C.LIBERICA

WHAT'S IN A NAME?
Arabica varieties are often named after the areas in which they were identified, so are known by many local names and spellings – for example the Geisha variety is also known as Gesha or Abyssinian.

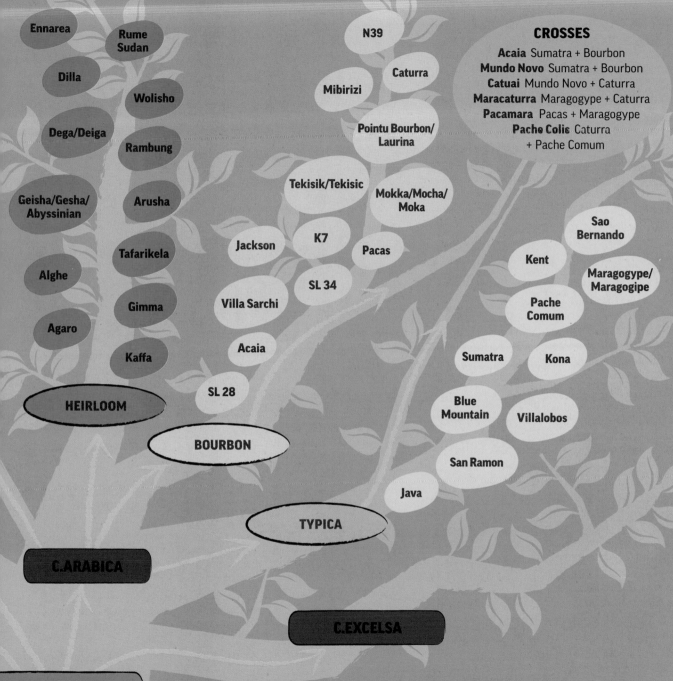

CROSSES
Acaia Sumatra + Bourbon
Mundo Novo Sumatra + Bourbon
Catuai Mundo Novo + Caturra
Maracaturra Maragogype + Caturra
Pacamara Pacas + Maragogype
Pache Colis Caturra
+ Pache Comum

GROWING AND HARVEST

The coffee tree is an evergreen. It grows in about 70 countries that offer suitable climates and altitudes. The trees are cultivated with care, and grow for about 3–5 years before they flower and produce fruit, known as coffee cherries.

Coffee cherries are picked from the tree during harvest – they contain two seeds, which after processing (pp20–23) become coffee beans. The main commercially grown coffee tree species are Arabica and Robusta (see pp12–13). Robustas are high-yielding and resistant to pests and diseases, producing coffee cherries with rustic flavour. They grow from cuttings that are planted in a nursery for a few months before they are moved out to the fields. Growers propagate Arabica trees from seed (see below), which produces coffee cherries that are generally superior in flavour.

GROWING ARABICA

Seeds are picked from ripe cherries grown on healthy Arabica trees ("mother trees"). These are planted and begin the growing process.

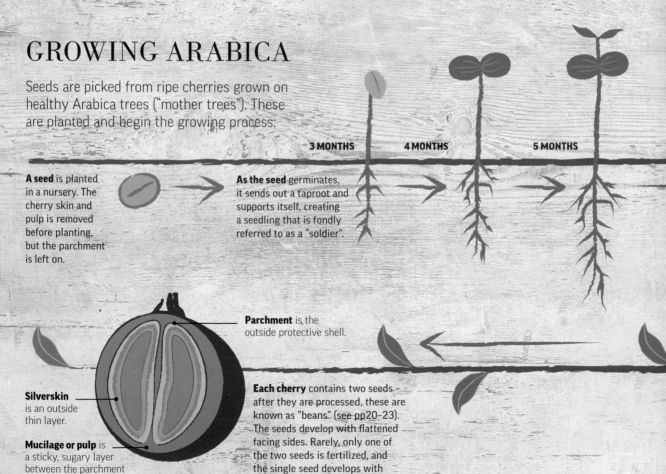

3 MONTHS   **4 MONTHS**   **5 MONTHS**

A seed is planted in a nursery. The cherry skin and pulp is removed before planting, but the parchment is left on.

As the seed germinates, it sends out a taproot and supports itself, creating a seedling that is fondly referred to as a "soldier".

Parchment is the outside protective shell.

Silverskin is an outside thin layer.

Mucilage or pulp is a sticky, sugary layer between the parchment and the cherry skin.

Each cherry contains two seeds – after they are processed, these are known as "beans" (see pp20–23). The seeds develop with flattened facing sides. Rarely, only one of the two seeds is fertilized, and the single seed develops with nothing to flatten it. This oval (or pea-shaped) speciality seed is known as a Peaberry.

GROWING CONDITIONS AFFECT THE QUALITY OF THE COFFEE – THE FLOWERS AND CHERRIES ARE SENSITIVE TO STRONG WINDS, SUNLIGHT, AND FROST

9 MONTHS

This "soldier" grows into a small tree with 12–16 leaves before it is planted in a field.

Soil protects the roots as the tree is replanted.

3–5 YEARS

The tree is left to mature for at least 3 years until the first flowering takes place.

These flowers mature into coffee cherries.

3–5 YEARS

The coffee cherries ripen on the branch, deepening in colour, until they are ready for harvest (see overleaf). The best-quality coffee cherries grow under shade or cloud cover. Near the equator, higher altitudes are needed to help reach the right temperature.

HARVEST TIME

Whatever the time of year, Arabica and Robusta are being harvested somewhere in the world. Some countries and regions harvest intensively once a year, others have two distinct harvest periods. Other areas have long seasons that last more or less all year round.

Depending on species and variety, the trees can grow several metres high, but are usually pruned to about 1.5m (5ft) high to facilitate picking, as this is mostly done by hand. Harvesters pick in one pass or several passes – stripping unripe cherries, overripe cherries, and everything in between in one go; or picking only the ripest cherries and returning to the same tree several times throughout the harvest season.

Some countries use machines that strip the branches or that gently shake the trees, causing the ripest cherries to fall off to be gathered.

TREES AND YIELD

One healthy Arabica tree produces about 1–5kg (2¼–11lb) of coffee cherries in a season, provided it is well cared for. You normally need about 5–6kg (11–13¼lb) of coffee cherries to make 1kg (2¼lb) of coffee beans. Whether stripped or selectively hand- or machine-picked, the coffee cherries are subjected to several stages of wet and dry processing (as shown on pp20–23), before the coffee beans are categorized according to quality.

UNRIPE ARABICA CHERRIES
There are 10–20 large round Arabica coffee cherries per cluster. They fall off the branch when ripe, so farmers carefully monitor and pick frequently. Trees can reach 3–4m (10–14ft) in height.

RIPE ROBUSTA CHERRIES
These trees reach up to 10–12m (33–40ft) in height. Pickers may use ladders to reach branches. There are 40–50 small round coffee cherries per cluster, which do not fall to the ground when ripe.

ARABICA VS ROBUSTA

The two main species of coffee tree have different botanical and chemical features and qualities. These dictate where they will naturally thrive and offer a sustainable crop, as well as how the coffee beans will be categorized and priced. These features also indicate a particular flavour profile.

FEATURES	ARABICA	ROBUSTA
Chromosomes An Arabica tree's genetic structure helps to explain why its coffee beans are varied and complex in flavour.	44	22
Root system Robustas have large, shallow roots that don't require the same depth and soil porosity as Arabicas.	**Deep** Farmers should allow 1.5m (5ft) between each tree, so that roots can spread comfortably.	**Shallow** At least 2m (6ft) is allowed between Robusta trees.
Ideal temperature Coffee trees are susceptible to frost. Farmers must plant them in areas that don't get too cold.	**15–25°C (60–80°F)** Arabica trees need a temperate climate to thrive.	**20–30°C (70–85°F)** Robusta trees grow well in hot temperatures.
Altitude and latitude Both species grow between the tropics of Cancer and Capricorn.	**900–2,000m (3,000–6,600ft) above sea level** High altitudes contribute to the required temperature and rainfall.	**0–900m (0–3,000ft) above sea level** Robusta trees don't require very cool temperatures, so grow at lower levels.
Rainfall range Rain encourages trees to flower, but too much and too little can damage the coffee flowers and cherries.	**1,500–2,500mm (60–100in)** A deep root system makes Arabicas capable of thriving when top level soil is dry.	**2,000–3,000mm (80–120in)** Robustas require frequent, heavy rainfall, as their root systems are relatively shallow.
Flowering period Both species flower following a rainfall, but there are contrasts depending on rain frequency.	**After rainfall** It is easy to predict when Arabica trees will flower, as they grow in regions with distinct wet seasons.	**Irregular** Robustas often grow in unstable, humid climates, and thus flower in a more irregular pattern.
From flower to cherry time The time it takes for flowers to mature into ripe cherries is different for each species.	**9 months** It takes Arabica trees less time to mature, allowing more time between cycles to prune and fertilize.	**10–11 months** Robusta trees require a relatively slow and prolonged period to mature. Harvest time is less intensive.
Oil content of beans Levels of oil are linked to aromatic intensity and so can give an indication of the quality.	**15–17%** High oil content lends a smooth and supple texture.	**10–12%** The low oil content of Robusta beans explains why Robusta espresso blends have a thick, stable crema.
Sugar content of beans The sugar level changes as the beans roast, affecting how we experience acidity and texture.	**6–9%**	**3–7%** Less sweet than Arabica beans, Robustas can taste "hard" and bitter, leaving a strong, long aftertaste.
Caffeine content of beans Caffeine is a natural pesticide, and so high levels can explain the hardiness of the coffee trees.	**0.8–1.4%**	**1.7–4%** This high content makes trees less susceptible to the diseases, fungi, and bugs that thrive in hot, wet climes.

Robusta beans

Arabica beans

PROCESSING

To become beans, coffee cherries need to be processed. Processing methods vary around the world, but the main methods are dry process (often referred to as "natural") or wet processes (either "washed" or "pulped natural").

Coffee cherries are at their sweetest when fully ripe, and should be processed within a few hours of harvest to preserve their quality. Processing can make or break a coffee; it can ruin even the most carefully grown and picked of cherries if it is not undertaken with care.

There are many variations to this practice. Some producers process the cherries themselves – if they have their own mills, they can retain control of the coffee until export. Other producers sell cherries to centralized "stations", who take care of the drying and/or milling process.

THE PREPARATION STAGE

The two initial processes differ, but share the same aim – to prepare the coffee cherry for the dry mill stage (see overleaf).

WET PROCESS

 1 Coffee cherries are poured into tanks filled with water. Usually both unripe and ripe cherries are poured in, but best practice is to choose only the ripest fruit.

 2 The cherries are sent through pulpers to remove the outer layers of the fruit (see p16). The machines strip off outer skin, but leave the mucilage intact. The skin is used for compost and fertilizer in fields and nurseries.

 3 The mucilage-covered beans are organized and separated into tanks, according to their weight.

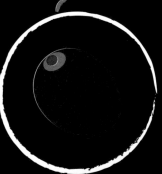

Coffee cherries
Fresh coffee cherries either go through an intensive washing process (above) or are rinsed and dried (below).

DRY PROCESS

NATURAL

 1 The whole coffee cherries are put through a quick wash or are floated in water. This separates any debris from the fruit.

 2 Producers transfer the cherries onto patios or raised beds where they spend around two weeks drying in the sun.

Under the sun, coffee cherries lose their bright colour and shrivel up.

PULPED NATURAL

④ The sugary mucilage-covered beans are carried or pumped onto drying patios and beds outside. They are spread out into 2.5–5cm (1–2in) layers, and are raked regularly to help them to dry evenly.

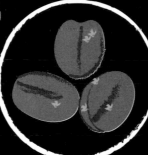

After a few days, a sugary sticky mucilage still covers the wet beans.

⑤ The coffee beans are left to dry for 7–12 days, according to the climate. If the coffee beans dry too quickly, it causes defects, limits shelf-life, and affects the flavour of the bean. In some places, beans are machine-dried in "guardiolas".

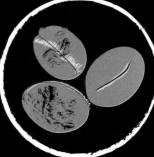

Once fully dried, the parchment-covered coffee beans look mottled with reddish or brown patches.

WASHED

④ The beans soak and ferment in these tanks for anything from 12–72 hours, until the mucilage breaks down and is washed off. There may be two soaks to bring out qualities in flavour or appearance.

⑤ Once all the pulp is removed, the clean parchment-covered beans are taken outside to dry on concrete or raised beds for 4–10 days.

⑥ Producers sort through the parchment-covered coffee beans by hand, removing damaged beans and turning them over to help with even drying.

Once dried, the parchment-covered coffee beans are uniform, clean, and a light beige colour.

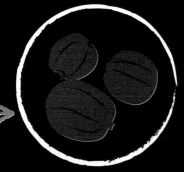

After they have dried in the sun, the cherries shrink further and turn brown.

IN GENERAL, THE WET PROCESSES HELP INHERENT FLAVOUR ATTRIBUTES OF THE COFFEE BEANS TO SHINE THROUGH

THE DRY MILL STAGE ⟶

THE DRY MILL STAGE

The dry natural coffee cherries and pulped natural/washed coffee beans rest for up to two months, before further processing at a dry mill.

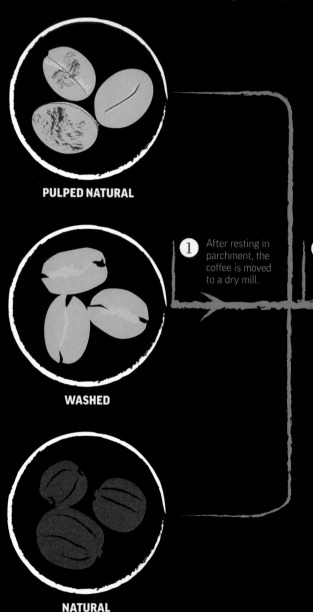

PULPED NATURAL

WASHED

NATURAL

PRODUCERS ASSIGN COFFEE BEANS INTO DIFFERENT CATEGORIES THAT INDICATE QUALITY

1 After resting in parchment, the coffee is moved to a dry mill.

2 The dry mill removes dried skin, parchment, and varying degrees of silverskin to reveal the green bean inside.

3 The coffee beans are placed on tables and conveyor belts and sorted into low- and high-quality by machine or by hand.

IN COFFEE, EVERYTHING HAS A BUYER, FROM THE CHEAPEST FLOOR SWEEPINGS TO THE TOP 1 PER CENT OF THE CROP

ONCE LOADED INTO CONTAINERS AND ONTO SHIPS, COFFEE BEANS TYPICALLY SPEND 2–4 WEEKS AT SEA ON THE WAY TO THEIR DESTINATION

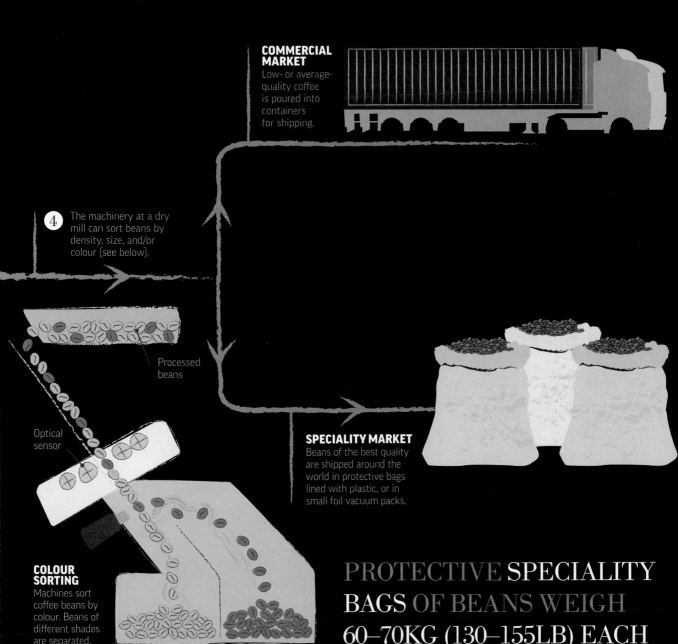

COMMERCIAL MARKET
Low- or average-quality coffee is poured into containers for shipping.

4 The machinery at a dry mill can sort beans by density, size, and/or colour (see below).

Processed beans

Optical sensor

SPECIALITY MARKET
Beans of the best quality are shipped around the world in protective bags lined with plastic, or in small foil vacuum packs.

COLOUR SORTING
Machines sort coffee beans by colour. Beans of different shades are separated.

PROTECTIVE SPECIALITY BAGS OF BEANS WEIGH 60–70KG (130–155LB) EACH

CUPPING

Many of us practise wine tasting, but wouldn't evaluate coffee in the same way. However, coffee tasting, known as "cupping", introduces you to unexpected and subtle flavours and helps you to identify and appreciate different coffees.

The coffee industry uses cupping to measure and control the quality of coffee beans – a cupping bowl provides a snapshot of the beans, whether it's a "micro lot" of a few bags, or a "large lot" of several containers. Coffee is usually scored on a scale from 0 to 100.

It's an industry-wide practice – from the exporters or importers, to the roasters and the baristas. Professional cuppers work for coffee companies, sourcing, tasting, and choosing the best coffees in the world. There are even national and international cupping competitions where the best cuppers compete for awards. Increasingly, producers and millers cup at the very beginning of a coffee's journey, too.

Cupping is easy to do at home – you don't have to be a tasting expert to know what you enjoy or dislike about a cup of coffee. Building up a vocabulary to describe flavours takes practice, but cupping a range of coffees from around the world soon introduces you to some broad flavour groupings that you can refine with time.

 WHAT DO I NEED?

Equipment
filter grinder
digital scale
250ml (9fl oz) heatproof cups, glasses, or bowls (If you do not have cups of the same size, use a digital scale or a measuring jug to ensure all cups are filled with the same volume of water)

Ingredients
coffee beans

HOW TO CUP

You can prepare just one cup of each coffee and explore its flavours, or try several side by side. You could cup with pre-ground coffee, but coffee tastes a lot fresher if you grind it yourself (see pp36–39).

1 Pour 12g (¼oz) of coffee beans into the first cup or glass. Grind each dose of beans to a medium grind, pouring the coffee back into its cup (see Tip).

2 Repeat with the other beans, but "clean" the grinder by grinding through a tablespoon of the next type of bean before you grind the beans you'll actually be cupping.

3 Once all the cups are full of ground coffee, smell them, taking note of how the aromas compare.

TIP
Grind separately, even if you are cupping multiples of the same bean for others to try, so that if there is one defective bean among the dose, it will be isolated in one cup and not spread across all of the cups.

4 Bring your water to the boil, then let it cool down to about 93–96°C (200–205°F). Pour the water over the coffee, making sure it is fully saturated. Fill the cup all the way to the top, or use a scale or measuring jug to ensure you use the correct volume of water to beans.

5 Leave the coffee to steep for 4 minutes. In this time you can evaluate the aroma of the "crust" – the floating layer of coffee grounds – taking care not to lift or disturb the cups. Perhaps you'll find the aromas to be stronger, weaker, better, or worse with some coffees compared to others.

6 After 4 minutes, use a spoon to gently stir the surface of the coffee three times, breaking the crust and settling the floating grounds. Rinse your spoon in hot water between every cup so you don't transfer any flavours from one bowl to another. Bring your nose to the cup as you break the crust to catch the release of aromas, and consider if the positive (or negative) attributes you noticed about the aroma in step 5 have changed.

7 Once all the crusts are broken, skim off the foam and floating particles with the help of two spoons, rinsing them with hot water between each skim.

8 When the coffee is cool enough to taste, dip your spoon in and slurp the coffee from the spoon into your mouth with a little air, which helps to spread the aromas to your olfactory system and the liquid across your palate. Consider the tactile sensations of the coffee as well as the flavour. How does it feel on your palate: does it seem thin, oily, soft, rough, elegant, drying, or creamy? How does it taste? Does it remind you of anything you have tasted before? Can you pick out any flavours of nuts, berries, or spices?

9 Go back and forth between coffees to compare. Revisit them as they cool and change, and take notes to help you to categorize, describe, and remember what you're tasting.

Water cools faster than you think, so pour as soon as it is the right temperature.

The crust should not collapse before you stir it – if it does, your water may be too cold or your roast too light.

Once the crust has been broken, use two spoons to help you skim the top of the coffee.

CONSIDER TACTILE IMPRESSIONS AS WELL AS THE FLAVOUR – DOES IT FEEL SUPPLE, SYRUPY, DELICATE, GRITTY? HOW DO AFTERTASTES COMPARE?

FLAVOUR APPRECIATION

Coffee offers an incredible range of complex aromas and flavours. Identify these subtleties of flavour to get the best from your coffee.

It is easy to improve your tasting palate with a little practice – the more you "cup" (see pp24–25), the easier it is to differentiate between coffees. These four flavour wheels act as prompts – keep them within easy reference to help you to identify and compare the aromas, flavours, textures, acidity levels, and aftertastes in coffee.

HOW TO USE THE WHEELS

First, identify key flavours using the large taster's wheel, honing in on specific profiles. Then, use the acidity, texture, and aftertaste wheels to help you to analyze physical sensations on the palate.

1 **Pour your cup of coffee** Breathe in through your nose, refer to the taster's wheel, and consider. Do you pick up hints of nuts, and, if so, are they reminiscent of hazelnut, peanut, or almond for example?

2 **Take a sip** Look at the taster's wheel again. Are there fruity notes, or nuances of spice? Ask yourself what is missing, as well as what is present. Identify broad groups, such as fruit, then move into more detail – decide if it's more like stone fruit or citrus. If citrus, is it lemon or grapefruit?

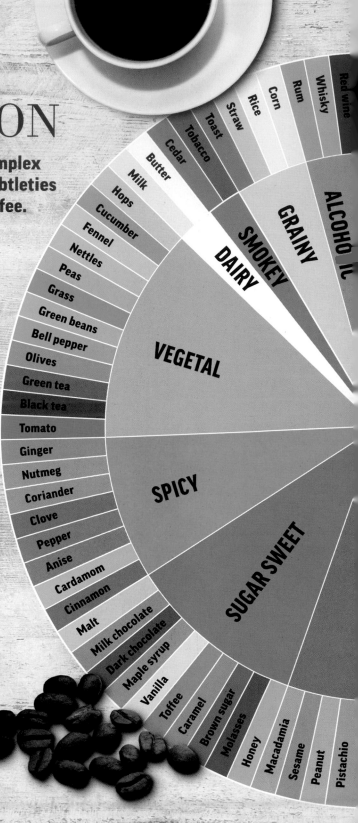

3 **Take another sip** A pleasant level of acidity adds freshness. Do you find flavours bright, intense, mellow, or flat?

4 **Focus on the texture** Coffee may be light or heavy. Does yours feel smooth and dense in the mouth, or light and refreshing?

5 **Swallow** Does the taste linger for long or disappear? Is it a neutral aftertaste, or bitter and unpleasant? Decide if any of the terms in the wheel apply to your coffee.

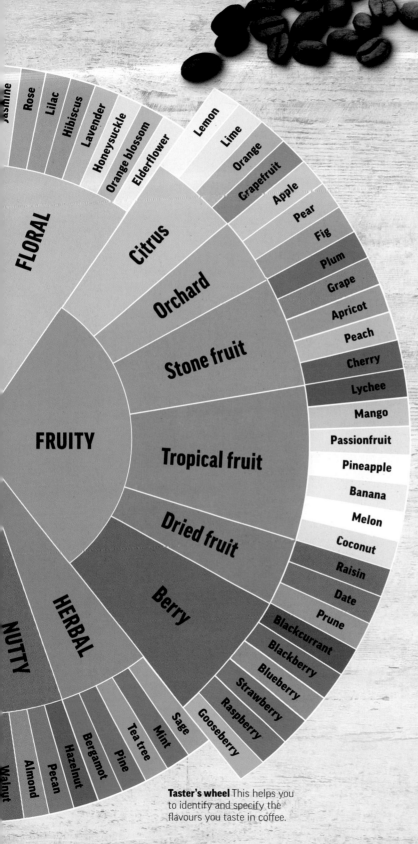

Taster's wheel This helps you to identify and specify the flavours you taste in coffee.

COFFEE KNOW-HOW

INDICATORS OF QUALITY

Coffee companies use specific language on packaging to describe their coffee – this can occasionally be confusing and conflicting, if not outright misleading. Understanding the terminology makes it easier to choose the coffee you want.

IDENTIFYING BEANS

Some coffee packaging only describes coffee as either Arabica or Robusta (the two main coffee species, see pp12–13). This is the equivalent of telling you only if a wine is white or red; you just don't have enough information to make an informed purchase. Although Robusta is generally inferior to Arabica, labels that tout only "pure Arabica" are also a misleading indicator of quality. Great Robustas do exist, but they are hard to find, so buying Arabica is often a safer bet – but there is a lot of poor Arabica out there, too. So what should discerning consumers expect to see on the labels?

The best-quality coffee beans are usually described with a high level of detail, such as by region, variety, processing method, and flavour (see p33). Consumers are growing in their understanding of good-quality coffee, and, as a result, roasters realize that the key to ensuring customer satisfaction is honesty and traceability.

BLENDS VS SINGLES

Both commercial and speciality companies often describe their coffee as either a "blend" or a "single origin". This description helps to explain the coffee's provenance – a blend is a mix of different coffee beans that creates a particular flavour profile, while a single-origin coffee is sourced from a single country or a single farm.

BLENDS
There are reasons why blends are popular, as they can create stable flavour profiles that remain consistent year-round. In the commercial sector, the ingredients and proportions in blends are closely guarded secrets, and the labels offer no indication of what the beans are or where they come from. Speciality roasters, however, clearly label and celebrate each component of a blend on the packaging – explaining the individual attributes of each bean and how the flavours complement and balance each other (see Sample Blend, opposite).

SINGLE ORIGINS
The term "single origin" is typically used to describe a coffee from a single country. However, identifying a coffee solely by country of origin is too broad – as it could still mean a blend of regions and farms within that country, and a mix of varieties and processes. It could also be of any level of quality – 100 per cent Brazilian, or any other country, does not mean that the coffee will be 100 per cent great. Equally, it gives you little indication of flavour as coffees from one region can taste very different to another.

A "BLEND" IS A MIX OF COFFEE BEANS FROM AROUND THE WORLD. A "SINGLE ORIGIN" REFERS TO A COFFEE FROM ONE COUNTRY, COOPERATIVE, OR FARM

When the speciality coffee sector use the term "single origin" on their packaging, they usually mean something more specific – coffees from a single farm, a single cooperative, a group of producers, or a producer and his family. These single-source coffees are often sold as limited or seasonal offerings, and may not be available year-round, but they will be sold for as long as the supply lasts and the coffee tastes its best.

RESPECTFUL PRACTICE

When coffee beans – regardless of whether they are single origin or blends – are grown and processed well, shipped carefully, and roasted with respect for the intrinsic flavours of the bean, it is a fantastic celebration of the nuances coffee can offer. Speciality coffee companies pride themselves on this practice, and, as a result, offer coffees of the highest quality.

SAMPLE BLEND

Roasters use blends to create varied flavours. Labels explain where each bean originates from and the quality it brings to the blend – as shown in this illustration of an excellent blend.

20% KENYA AA WASHED SL 28
BRIGHT ACIDITY
BLACKCURRANT
CHERRY

THE BLEND
A COMPLEX BLEND OF FRUIT, NUTS, AND CHOCOLATE WITH A SWEET AFTERTASTE AND SYRUPY TEXTURE

30% NICARAGUA WASHED CATURRA
SWEET
CARAMEL
ROASTED HAZELNUT
MILK CHOCOLATE

50% EL SALVADOR PULPED NATURAL BOURBON
BALANCED
PLUM
APPLE
TOFFEE

CHOOSING AND STORING

Finding good-quality coffee to brew at home has never been easier – even without a specialist coffee shop close to home. Many coffee roasters sell online and offer brewing equipment and tips on how to make the most of their beans.

CHOOSING

WHERE TO BUY

Supermarkets rarely treat coffee as the fresh product that it is, so you will have more luck buying good, fresh beans from a local or an online shop that specializes in coffee. However, navigating through all the options and exotic descriptions can be a difficult task. Do a bit of research before deciding who to trust as your coffee supplier. Look for a few key points such as how the beans are described and packaged, rely on your taste buds, and be open to compare and experiment until you find the coffee provider that gives you the quality you want.

CONTAINERS

If you buy loose beans from a shop, ensure you know when the beans were roasted. Coffee is best protected in containers with lids – unless stored airtight it loses its vibrancy after a few days.

SCALES

Buying less means buying fresh. If you can, buy only the amount of beans you need to brew for a few days or a week at a time. You can often buy as little as 100g (3½oz).

WHAT'S ON THE BAG?

A lot of coffee is sold in attractive packaging that actually offers very little useful information about the product you buy. The more relevant information you find, the better the odds of buying a good-quality product.

One-way valve Fresh coffee expels CO_2 as a bi-product of the roasting process. If left unprotected, CO_2 escapes, oxygen enters, and complex aromatics are lost. A bag with a valve allows you to seal the coffee so that the CO_2 escapes but oxygen cannot stale it.

Date The bag should have a "roasted and packed" date on it, and not just a "best-before" date. Most commercial coffee companies will not tell you when the coffee was roasted or packed, but instead operate with best-before dates that are anything from 12 to 24 months into the future. This is not in the best interest of the coffee, nor you, the consumer.

Provenance The label should tell you which species and/or variety the coffee is, where it was grown, and whether it is a blend or single source (see pp30–31).

Roast level An indication of roast level is useful, but the language used to communicate roast is not standardized. "Medium roast" could be any shade of brown depending on who you ask. "Filter roast" generally indicates something on the lighter end, while "espresso roast" is a darker version. However, it is not uncommon to find filter beans that are darker from one roaster than an espresso roast from another. A knowledgeable retailer can advise you on which roast you might like.

07-03-14

FINCA LA SAETA DE CORAZON PITALITO, HUILA, COLOMBIA
Margarita Maria Salazar Huertas

100% CATURRA
SEMI-SHADE GROWN

LIGHT–MEDIUM ROAST
SUITABLE FOR FILTER-STYLE BREWING

This beautiful, **fully-washed coffee** is from Señorita Salazar's two-hectare farm outside Pitalito, with an altitude of 1,700m (5,577ft) above sea level. It shines in the cup, with **bright lemongrass acidity**, rose hip, green apple, and honey notes, and a **delicate, creamy texture**.

COFFEE OBSESSION ROASTING COMPANY

Traceability Ideally, you should be able to find the name of a cooperative, washing station, hacienda, finca, or fazenda, as well as the name of the farm owner or manager. The more traceable a coffee is, the better are the chances that you are buying something of quality that was traded at a sustainable price and has been handled with care all the way from producer to retailer.

Expected flavour There should be information on how the coffee was processed and what the flavour should be like. Even information on altitude or presence of shade trees can be indicators as to the quality of the beans inside.

THE PRICE GAP BETWEEN CHEAP COFFEE AND ETHICALLY SOURCED COFFEE IS FAR LESS PROFOUND THAN MANY WOULD THINK

PACKAGING

The main enemies of coffee are oxygen, heat, light, moisture, and strong odours. Avoid buying beans that are stored in open containers or hoppers unless the containers look clean, are protected with lids or sneeze guards, and you see a roast date. Unless carefully managed, these containers do nothing to preserve the quality of their contents. Look for coffee in opaque, airtight bags that have a one-way valve on them. This is a small plastic disc that lets the CO_2 from the beans out of the bag, but prevents oxygen from entering. Kraft paper bags offer minimal protection so treat these beans as loose-weight coffee. Avoid coffee from bags or bricks that are vacuum-sealed, as this coffee would have completely de-gassed and gone stale before packaging. Buy as fresh as you can, as even a week after roasting can be too old.

IS EXPENSIVE ALWAYS BEST?

The cheapest coffee is never high-quality coffee. It was probably not sourced at a price that covered the cost of production. You should also be wary of coffees where a high price feeds into a marketing gimmick, such as expensive, and frequently fraudulent, animal-faeces coffee, or exotic island coffee where you might be paying a premium for the marketing of the brand rather then a superior flavour. The difference in price between poor- and high-quality coffee is often very small, making a truly great cup of coffee one of the most affordable luxuries you can get.

TIP
An increasing number of quality-focused cafés sell single-serve coffee brewers, such as AeroPresses, alongside their coffees. Ask your barista for recommendations and guidance for using your equipment like a pro.

STORING

Buying whole beans and investing in a home grinder is one of the best ways to make sure you get fresher coffee at home. Pre-ground coffee will become stale in a matter of hours, but whole beans will stay fresh for a few days, or even up to several weeks, if properly sealed. Attempt to buy only what you need for a week or two of drinking. Buy whole beans, invest in a manual or electric home burr grinder (see pp36–39), and grind only what you need for each brew.

STORING DOS
Store the beans in an airtight container, in a dry, dark place, away from strong odours. If the bag containing the beans does not fulfill these criteria, place the bag in a tupperware or similar container.

STORING DON'TS
Avoid storing your coffee beans in the fridge, but if you must preserve your beans for longer, freeze them and thaw only what you need to brew each time. Do not re-freeze beans that have already been thawed.

COMPARING STALE AND FRESH COFFEES
Fresh, well roasted coffee should be intensely and sweetly aromatic; free of harsh, acidic, or metallic notes. The presence of CO_2 is a very good indicator of freshness. In this visual comparison, two cups have been brewed using the "cupping" method (see pp24–25).

Fresh coffee As water reacts with the CO_2 in fresh coffee, foam and bubbles form a "bloom" that gently settles after a minute or two.

Stale coffee This coffee contains very little or no CO_2 for the water to react with, so it forms a flat, dull lid. The grounds can also be very dry and difficult to saturate.

GRINDING

Many of us invest in expensive coffee-brewing equipment, but don't realise that one of the easiest ways to vastly improve the quality of the coffee we make and to achieve the correct texture, is to grind fresh coffee beans with a good grinder.

THE RIGHT GRINDER

There is a difference between grinders for espresso and grinders for filter-style brews, so make sure you buy one designed for your preferred method, as shown opposite and on pages 38–39. However, there are some key choices that affect both types of grinders.

Grinders with blades are most commonly available, and usually run for as long as you hold down the "on" button. Even if you are using a timer to measure how long to grind for and how fine to go, you will find it hard to replicate accurately the size of ground coffee particles from one cup to another, especially if you vary the amount of coffee each time. Blade grinders also lead to a lot of grit at the bottom of your cup, particularly if you brew with a French press. An advantage is that they are generally quite affordable. If you

would like to step it up a notch, invest a little more money in a grinder with "burrs", conical or flat (see below), that will crush the beans into particles of a more uniform size and allow for more even extractions. Some grinders have "stepped" adjustments that lock into set grind sizes; others are "stepless" and allow you to adjust in tiny increments. Burr grinders do not have to be expensive, especially if they are the manual, hand-cranked variety. However, if you want to spend a bit more or plan to grind large quantities of coffee each day, choose an electric one. They often have a timer function that you can use as a way of dosing how much coffee you grind. Keep in mind that the coarser a grinder is set, the less time it takes to grind through a 30g (1oz) dose of beans, and the finer it is set, the longer it takes to grind the same amount.

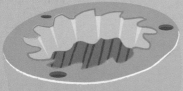

CONICAL BURRS
These burrs are more resilient than flat ones, but they need replacing after you have ground around 750–1,000kg (1,650–2,000lb) coffee.

FLAT BURRS
Grinders with flat burrs are usually cheaper, but need replacing after you have ground around 250–600kg (550–1,300lb) of coffee.

FILTER-STYLE GRINDERS

These grinders are cheaper than espresso grinders. They can be adjustable, but will not normally grind fine enough for espresso. They also rarely have a dosing, or measuring, mechanism.

As explained opposite, avoid buying the ones that use whirling blades to chop the coffee into pieces, as these are hard to control and often create fine dust that will over-extract, as well as several large chunks of bean that will barely extract at all. This can result in an imbalance in flavour that even good beans and correct brewing can't fix.

Hopper
Choose a grinder with a hopper that suits the volume of coffee you wish to grind on a regular basis.

Timer dial
Some grinders have a timer function and switch off automatically.

Grind adjustment
Choose a grinder that you can easily adjust without needing to dismantle many parts.

Drawer
Avoid storing coffee in the drawer, and grind only as much as you need per brew.

ELECTRIC FILTER GRINDER
Convenient and quick to use, make sure you clean electric filter grinders with special cleaning tablets on a regular basis.

FILTER-STYLE HAND GRINDER
These require a little patience and muscle, but are great if you require only a small amount or you'd like fresh coffee without access to electricity.

ESPRESSO-STYLE GRINDERS

Engineered to grind very finely, espresso grinders are adjustable in small increments, and often portion out coffee for each dose. They are heavier than filter-style grinders, with solid motors and a higher price point, but they are an essential investment if you want to produce really good espresso at home.

Hopper
Most grinders have hoppers that hold 1kg (2¼lb) beans at a time, but to keep your coffee fresh, fill with only as much as you can brew in two days.

Stepless adjustment
This helps to produce grounds at the exact particle size you prefer.

Burr
Good espresso grinders should have flat or conical burrs (see p36).

Doser
Some grinders have digital timer functions so you can grind what you need per shot. This reduces waste.

ESPRESSO GRINDER

You will need a grinder designed specifically for espresso and it should only be used for espresso. It takes time and beans to "dial a grinder in" (set your grinder up correctly) to brew a great shot. Adjusting it to go from espresso to filter and back again during the course of a day will take a long time – and waste a lot of coffee.

On/off button
If you don't have a grinder with a doser, simply use your on/off button to stop grinding.

WHICH GRIND FOR WHICH METHOD?

METHOD	GRIND

Ibrik coffee pot The texture for making Turkish coffee in an ibrik should be almost powdery, so that the maximum flavour gets extracted in the brewing process. Most grinders won't grind fine enough for this – you need a special hand grinder for this purpose.

Super-fine grind

CLOSE-UP

Espresso machine Espresso is the least-forgiving brew method, and as such the grounds' particle size must be just the right fine grind, allowing a balanced shot to be extracted.

Fine grind

CLOSE-UP

Filter Medium-ground coffee is suitable for many brewing methods, including filter pour-over, cloth brewer, stove-top pot, electric filter-brew, and cold dripper. Within limits, you can increase or decrease the dosage of coffee you use to get the result you prefer.

Medium–coarse grind

CLOSE-UP

French press These brewers have no filtration system, so water has time to penetrate the cell structure of coarser ground beans. This helps dissolve pleasant solubles while helping to avoid excessive bitterness.

Coarse grind

CLOSE-UP

TESTING THE WATER

Water makes up 98–99 per cent of a cup of coffee, so the quality of water you brew with has a major impact on the flavour.

WHAT'S IN YOUR WATER?

Water for brewing coffee should be odourless and clear in colour. The combination of minerals, salts, and metals that can affect the brew may not be perceptible by sight or taste. Some areas have water that is clean and soft, while others have hard water that may contain chemical flavours such as chlorine or ammonia. If the water in your area is too hard, it is in essence already saturated with minerals and may under-extract the coffee, leaving you with a thinner, weaker brew. You may find it necessary to use a higher dose of coffee or a finer grind to compensate for this. Equally, water that is too soft or has had all minerals removed can over-extract your coffee, dissolving undesirable elements from the bean and making your coffee taste bitter or sour.

QUALITY CHECK

Test water quality in your own kitchen. Brew two bowls of coffee using the cupping method (as shown on pp24–25). Keep the beans, grind, and brew recipe the same, but brew one with tap water and the other with bottled water. Taste them side by side, and you may notice flavours in the coffee that you've never noticed before.

Carbon filter
Activated carbon absorbs impurities.

WATER FILTER Replace the filter regularly (when around 100 litres/22 gallons water has been filtered, or more often if you have hard water).

FILTER IT

If your tap water is too hard and you don't want to use bottled water for brewing coffee, investing in a simple home water filter can give you good results. You can buy filtration kits that are installed on your water line, or a simple water jug with a replaceable carbon filter (as shown above). The difference in flavour between water with and without the optimum mineral content is quite stark, and is often a surprise to most consumers. Changing from tap to bottled or filtered water is one of the easiest ways to improve the quality of coffee at home.

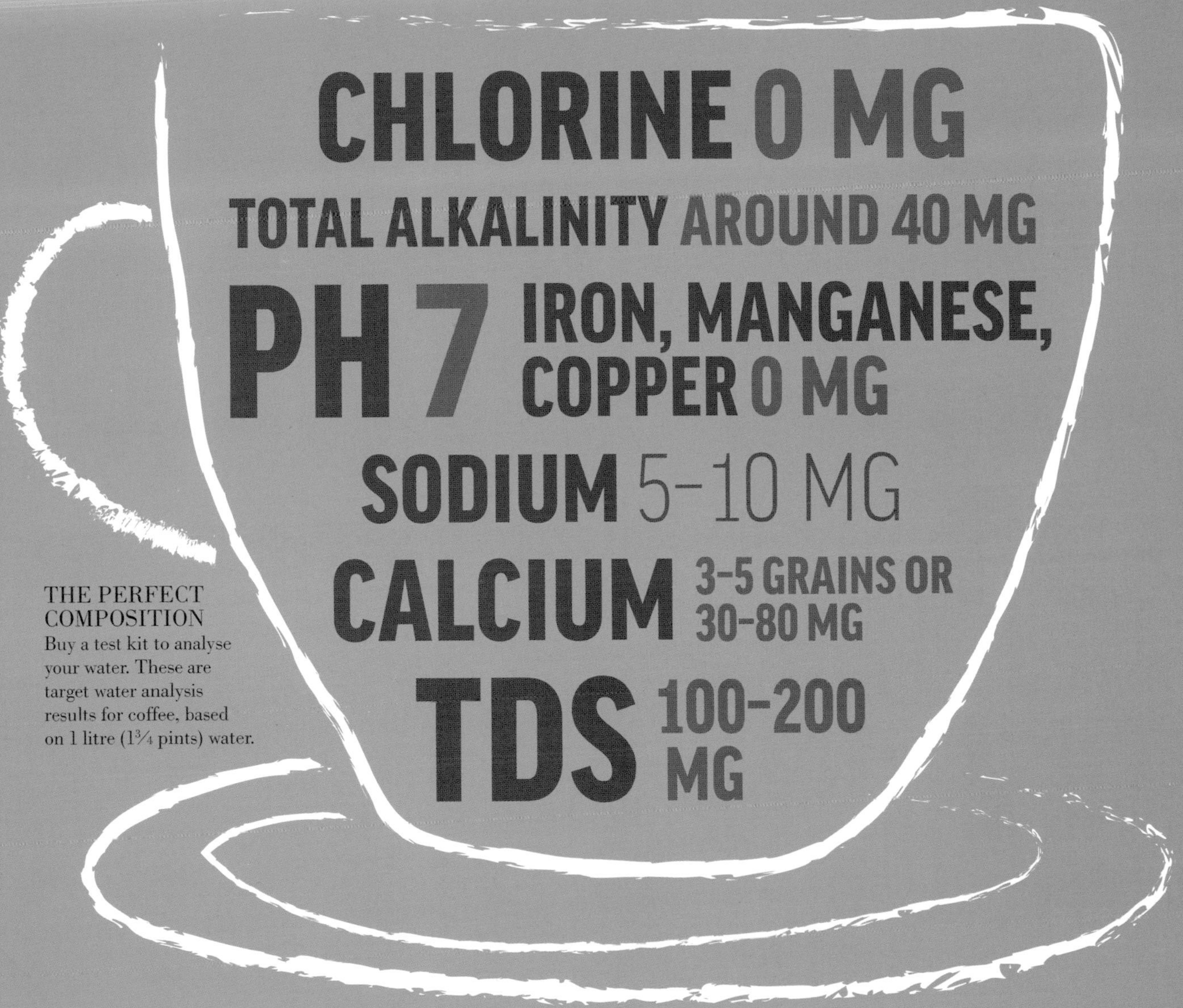

CHLORINE 0 MG

TOTAL ALKALINITY AROUND 40 MG

PH 7 IRON, MANGANESE, COPPER 0 MG

SODIUM 5-10 MG

CALCIUM 3-5 GRAINS OR 30-80 MG

TDS 100-200 MG

THE PERFECT COMPOSITION
Buy a test kit to analyse your water. These are target water analysis results for coffee, based on 1 litre (1¾ pints) water.

WHAT DOES IT ALL MEAN?

The most common term used to describe water quality in relation to the extraction of coffee is Total Dissolved Solids (TDS), measured in mg/L or parts per million (ppm). This is the combined amount of organic and inorganic compounds in your water. "Grains of hardness" is another term, used to describe the amount of calcium ions present. The pH should be neutral: if it's too high or too low it can cause the coffee to have a flat or unpleasant flavour.

BREWING ESPRESSO

Espresso is the only method that brews coffee using pump pressure. When you brew coffee with an espresso machine, the water temperature is kept below boiling point, which helps to avoid scalding the coffee.

WHAT IS ESPRESSO?

There are many theories and practices when it comes to brewing espresso, from the classic Italian approach to the American adaptations, and the Scandinavian versions to the Antipodean interpretations. Irrespective of which approach you prefer and follow, it's useful to remember that espresso, at its core, is just a brewing method as well as the name of a beverage. Many people also use the term "espresso" as a way of describing a roast colour, but in fact, you can brew espresso using any level of roast, and any bean or blend that you prefer.

PREPARING THE MACHINE

In addition to your machine manufacturer's recommendations, here are a few guidelines that can help make the road to a good home espresso a bit smoother.

 WHAT DO I NEED?

Equipment
espresso machine
espresso grinder
dry cloth
tamper
tamping mat
cleaning powder
cleaning tools

Ingredients
roasted coffee beans (rested)

1 Fill the clean espresso machine with fresh water and the grinder with beans that have been given a week or two to rest and de-gas since roasting. Allow the machine and portafilter to become thoroughly warmed up.

2 Wipe the basket of the portafilter clean with a dry cloth, so that none of the coffee grounds in the machine are re-brewed.

THEORIES ABOUND ABOUT THE **RIGHT ROAST AND BEAN**, BUT AT ITS CORE, **ESPRESSO** IS JUST A **BREWING METHOD**

TIP

Good espresso takes practice. Try using an electric scale and small measuring glasses to help get proportions right, taking notes as you go. Trust your taste, and experiment to find out what you like.

3 Flush some water through the group head to stabilize the temperature and clean any old coffee residue off the shower screen.

4 Grind the coffee and dose between 16g (½oz) and 20g (¾oz) into the basket, according to its size and your preferred recipe.

BREWING THE SHOT

Brewing great coffee repeatedly and consistently can be very challenging, and making espresso at home takes a lot more effort than any other brewing method. For those who choose to invest in the machinery required to do a good job, it is a hobby as much as a daily drinking ritual.

Coffee for espresso must be very finely ground, allowing the water to extract from a larger surface area. The result is a small, intense, viscous drink with a foam called crema, that highlights all the good, but potentially also the bad, qualities of the bean, roast, and preparation.

1 Distribute the coffee evenly by gently shaking the portafilter or tapping it gently on the counter. Use a designated distribution tool (as shown) if you prefer.

2 Use a tamper that fits the size of your basket. Keeping it level to the edges of the basket, press the coffee down with a firm push to create a solid puck of even thickness. It is not necessary to apply excessive force, to tap the portafilter, or to tamp repeatedly.

3 The goal is to push all the coffee down and create a firm, even bed of grounds that will withstand the pressure of the water and allow the water to flow through and extract the coffee evenly.

TIP
Don't press down as you level the bed of ground coffee – use a tool or your finger and move the mound of coffee from side to side and up and down until you have loosely filled in all of the gaps.

BREWING ESPRESSO CAN BECOME
A HOBBY OR A DAILY DRINKING
RITUAL. IT REQUIRES SOME WORK,
BUT IS GREAT FUN TO MASTER

TIP
You may have to throw away several shots each day before you grind your coffee to the right coarseness and get a shot you are happy with. Check out the common pitfalls to brewing the perfect espresso on p46.

4 Insert the portafilter into the group head, and immediately activate the pump to brew, using either the volumetric settings for two shots of espresso or the free-flow button, which you switch off when you reach the desired volume.

5 Place a warmed espresso cup under the spouts (or two cups if you wish to split the shot into two singles).

6 The coffee should appear after 5–8 seconds, dripping and flowing with a deep brown or golden colour that lightens as the brew progresses and the solubles are washed out. You should extract around 50ml (1¹⁄₂fl oz) in 25–30 seconds, including crema.

IS IT PERFECT?

A well-brewed espresso should have a smooth layer of crema (see p44) with a deep golden brown colour, free from any large bubbles and pale or broken spots. The crema needs to be a couple of millimeters thick once settled, and should not dissipate too quickly. The taste should be balanced between sweet and acidic, and the texture should be smooth and creamy, leaving you with a pleasant lingering aftertaste. You should be able to taste the qualities of the coffee itself over the roast or brewing technique – be it a chocolatey Guatemalan, a nutty Brazilian, or a blackcurrant-like Kenyan.

WHAT COULD GO WRONG?

If you have extracted more than 50ml (1¹/₂fl oz) at the given time (see p45), it could be because:
• the grind size is too coarse and/or
• the dose is too low

If you have extracted less than 50ml (1¹/₂fl oz), it could be because:
• the grind is too fine and/or
• you are using too much coffee

If a coffee is too acidic and sour, it could be because:
• the water in the machine is too cold
• the beans are too lightly roasted
• the grind is too coarse
• the dose is too low

If an espresso is too bitter, it could be because:
• the water is too hot
• the machine is dirty
• the beans are roasted too dark
• the grinder burrs are too dull
• the grind is too fine
• the dose is too high

Well-brewed espresso

Imperfect espresso

CLEANING THE MACHINE

Coffee is made up of oils, particles, and other solubles. If you don't keep your equipment clean, these substances can build up and impart a bitter, ashy taste to coffee. Rinse with water between shots, and backflush with specialized cleaning solution daily, or as often as is possible.

TIP
Use a small clean brush to clean off the rubber gasket in the group head of your machine. To make sure your gasket stays in place, keep the portafilter locked into the machine even when you are not using it.

2 Knock the spent puck out of the portafilter, and wipe it clean with a dry cloth.

1 Set the cup to the side, and remove the portafilter from the group head.

3 Flush the group head with some water to remove any coffee stuck on the screen, rinsing off the spouts at the same time. Place the portafilter back in the group head to keep it warm for the next shot.

MILK MATTERS

A good cup of coffee deserves to be enjoyed black, without milk, sugar, or other flavourings; but nobody can deny that milk is a perfect pairing that is enjoyed by millions every day. Steam your milk to accentuate its naturally sweet flavour.

TYPES OF MILK

You can steam any type of milk you like – full-fat, semi-skimmed, or skimmed, but there are differences in the taste and texture. Low-fat milks produce a lot of foam but might feel a bit dry and crisp. Full-fat milks might produce less foam but will be smooth and creamy. Even non-dairy milks like soy, almond, hazelnut, or lactose-free milk will steam and produce foam. Rice milk does not produce much foam, but can be a substitute for those with nut allergies. Some of these milks seem to heat quicker and the foam might be less stable or smooth than with dairy.

STEAMING

Practise with larger volumes of milk than you might need to prepare your drink. This gives you time to experiment before the temperature gets too high and you have to stop. A 1-litre (1³/₄ pint) pitcher, half full with milk, is best to start with, as long as the steam wand on your machine reaches the surface of the milk. If it doesn't, try a 750ml (1¹/₄ pint) or 500ml (16fl oz) pitcher. Any smaller than this can make it tricky, as the milk heats up too fast for you to get used to the movement of the milk and the rate at which to add air.

1 Use a steaming pitcher that tapers slightly at the top as you will need room for the milk to swirl, expand, and foam up without spilling. Start with cold, fresh milk, and fill the pitcher no more than half full, as shown.

2 Purge any water or milk residue out of your steam arm until only clean steam comes out. To avoid spilling, wrap a dedicated cloth around the steam nozzle to catch any water. Take care to keep your fingers away from the nozzle so as not to burn them.

AS TINY POCKETS OF AIR AND STEAM ARE ADDED TO THE MILK, YOU WILL HEAR GENTLE, CONTROLLED SLURPING NOISES

TIP

If you don't want to waste a lot of milk to practice on, you can use water with a small drop of dishwashing liquid to mimic the process until you're comfortable with the concept of adding air and spinning the milk in a controlled manner.

3 Hold the pitcher level and upright. Position the steam arm inside the pitcher at an angle, slightly off-centre but not touching the sides. The nozzle should be only just submerged.

4 If you're right-handed, hold the handle of the pitcher in your right hand and use your left to turn the steam on. Don't hesitate to turn it up quite high. If you don't use enough steam pressure, you won't create any bubbles and the milk will make a loud, screeching sound. Move your left hand to the bottom of the steam pitcher. It will now function as your temperature gauge.

5 The direction of the steam pressure should push the milk around in circles. The longer you maintain the slurping noise, the more foam you will generate. As the foam increases, it acts as a sound buffer and reduces the noise. As the noise gets gentler, the bubbles get smaller creating a denser foam.

TECHNIQUE CONTINUES ➞

STEAMING (continued)

6 As the milk warms, it expands and rises up above the nozzle, cutting off the air. For lots of foam, lower the pitcher so the nozzle remains at the surface. For less, let the milk rise above the nozzle. Maintain the swirling of the liquid and beat the big bubbles into smaller bubbles to create a smoother, denser foam.

7 Add air only while the milk is still cold. Once you feel the base of the pitcher reach body temperature, stop adding air – any bubbles formed beyond about 37°C (99°F) are harder to mix into a smooth foam. If you add air in as soon as the steam is switched on, you should have plenty of time to create as much foam as you'd like.

8 Swirl the milk until the bottom of the pitcher becomes too hot to touch. Move your left hand away, give the process another 3 seconds, and turn the steam off. This should result in milk at about 60–65°C (140–150°F). If you hear a deep, rumbling noise, you are boiling the milk and it will taste eggy or porridge-like, not ideal for coffee.

9 Set the pitcher down to the side. Use a damp cloth to clean the steam wand, and purge for a few seconds into the cloth to ensure that any milk residue on the inside of the wand is expelled. If there are any big bubbles on the surface of the milk, a few seconds of rest will weaken them. Gently tap the jug on the countertop to burst them.

10 Once the big bubbles stop appearing, swirl the milk around in the jug until you achieve a glossy, shiny texture of milk and foam combined. If you are left with an "island" of dry foam that floats around in the middle, gently slosh the milk from side to side to try to incorporate it, then swirl again in a circular motion.

11 By swirling to keep the milk and foam mixed right up until the point where you pour it into your cup, you will not need a spoon to get the foam out, and with some practice, you will also be able to create latte art.

TIP
There is no need to move the milk pitcher vigorously at any stage. The force and direction of the steam should do all the work, so just keep a steady position and controlled angle of the steam arm and jug.

LATTE ART

Your milk must be smooth and have a dense foam, but it should look beautiful, too! Latte art takes practice, but once mastered, it'll spruce up a cup of coffee. Many designs start with a basic heart, so start with that and see where it takes you.

HEART

This design suits a slightly thicker layer of milk foam and so is a good choice to try on cappuccinos.

1 Start by pouring the steamed milk into the middle of the crema from about 5cm (2in) above the cup, letting the crema rise and stretch the "canvas".

2 Once the cup is about half full, quickly lower the pitcher down to the cup while maintaining your pour and its position in the middle. You should see a circle of milky foam start to spread out into the cup.

3 When the cup is nearly full, lift your pitcher back up and pour a line through the circle, allowing the flow of the milk to pull it out into a heart shape.

POURING LIKE A PRO

If you pour milk from too great a height, it lifts up the crema, leaving very little white on the surface. Conversely, if you pour the milk when your pitcher is too close to the cup, it drowns the crema in white foam. If you pour too slowly, you won't get the movement you need to create a pattern; if too fast, the crema and milk will mix uncontrollably. Practise pouring from a 500ml (16fl oz) pitcher into a large cup, until you find the perfect balance between height and speed.

ROSETTA

Often seen on caffè lattes and flat whites, the rosetta works best with a slightly thinner foam.

1 Follow step 1 for the heart, opposite, then once the cup is about half full, quickly lower the pitcher down to the cup. Start rocking it gently from side to side in a "tick tock" motion.

2 Let the flow of milk spill out in a zigzag-like pattern. When your cup is nearly full, start moving the pitcher backwards to create increasingly smaller zigzag shapes.

3 When you have finished creating your zigzags, pour a line straight down the middle to finish, holding your pitcher from a little more height.

SWIRL THE JUG CONTINUOUSLY, RIGHT UP TO THE POINT OF POURING, TO KEEP THE FOAM AND MILK FROM SEPARATING

TIP

As well as free-pouring latte art designs like the heart, rosetta, and tulip, some enjoy etching. This involves creating designs, such as chasing hearts (pictured, far right), by pulling a thin utensil through dollops of milk foam.

TULIP

The tulip is an advanced version of the heart (see p52) that uses a stop-and-start technique.

1 Start as you would for the heart, pouring a small circle of white into the middle of the cup.

2 Stop your pour and start again 1cm (½in) behind the first pour, carefully moving the pitcher forwards as the foam comes out, pushing the first circle forwards and out to the sides in a crescent shape.

3 Repeat until you have as many "leaves" as you would like. Finish with a small heart on top, pulling the line down through the leaves to create the stem.

ELABORATE Adapt the basic designs to create (clockwise from top left): multi-tulips, chasing hearts, swans, rosetta hearts.

COFFEES OF THE WORLD
AFRICA

ETHIOPIA

The complex mix of species and varieties that are native to Ethiopia gives these coffees their potential for unique flavours. They are famed for unusually distinct and elegant floral, herbal, and citrus notes.

UNRIPE COFFEE CHERRIES
When ripened (see pp16–17), coffee cherries are picked once, twice, or three times a week.

Ethiopia is often hailed as the birthplace of Arabica coffee, although recent studies indicate that South Sudan may also have the right to claim this title. Ethiopia doesn't have a lot of coffee farms – they are either referred to as garden, forest, semi-forest, or plantation – but around 15 million people are involved in the coffee-production process, from picking to export. Coffee grows wild, produced largely by subsistence farmers, who sell it only for a few months every year.

Ethiopia has a biodiversity of species and varieties that is not found elsewhere, with many yet to be identified. Due to the mix of Heirloom varieties grown – such as Moka and Geisha – coffee beans from Ethiopia often lack uniformity in size and shape.

Climate change is eradicating wild species of coffee trees that may hold genetic keys to coffee's survival. The huge genetic range of local Heirloom varieties will be key to securing the future of coffee worldwide.

ETHIOPIAN COFFEE KEY FACTS

PERCENTAGE OF WORLD MARKET: 5%

HARVEST: OCTOBER–DECEMBER

MAIN TYPES: ARABICA NATIVE HEIRLOOM VARIETIES

PROCESSES: WASHED AND NATURAL

PRODUCTION IN 2012: 8 MILLION BAGS

WORLD RANKING AS A PRODUCER: 5TH LARGEST COFFEE PRODUCER IN THE WORLD

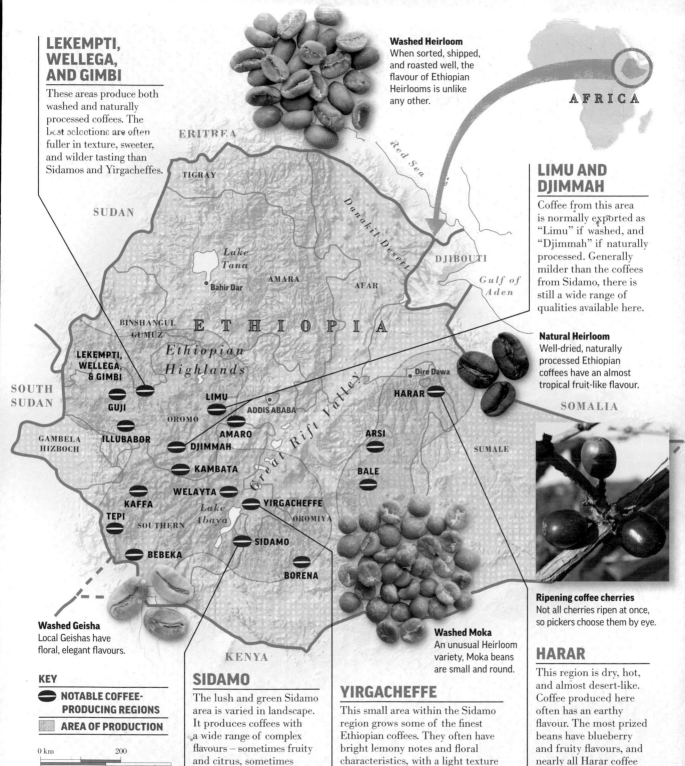

LEKEMPTI, WELLEGA, AND GIMBI

These areas produce both washed and naturally processed coffees. The best selections are often fuller in texture, sweeter, and wilder tasting than Sidamos and Yirgacheffes.

Washed Heirloom
When sorted, shipped, and roasted well, the flavour of Ethiopian Heirlooms is unlike any other.

AFRICA

LIMU AND DJIMMAH

Coffee from this area is normally exported as "Limu" if washed, and "Djimmah" if naturally processed. Generally milder than the coffees from Sidamo, there is still a wide range of qualities available here.

Natural Heirloom
Well-dried, naturally processed Ethiopian coffees have an almost tropical fruit-like flavour.

Ripening coffee cherries
Not all cherries ripen at once, so pickers choose them by eye.

Washed Geisha
Local Geishas have floral, elegant flavours.

KEY

🔵 **NOTABLE COFFEE-PRODUCING REGIONS**

▨ **AREA OF PRODUCTION**

0 km   200

0 miles   200

SIDAMO

The lush and green Sidamo area is varied in landscape. It produces coffees with a wide range of complex flavours – sometimes fruity and citrus, sometimes nutty and herbal.

YIRGACHEFFE

This small area within the Sidamo region grows some of the finest Ethiopian coffees. They often have bright lemony notes and floral characteristics, with a light texture and a well-balanced sweetness.

Washed Moka
An unusual Heirloom variety, Moka beans are small and round.

HARAR

This region is dry, hot, and almost desert-like. Coffee produced here often has an earthy flavour. The most prized beans have blueberry and fruity flavours, and nearly all Harar coffee is naturally processed.

Map labels: ERITREA, TIGRAY, SUDAN, Lake Tana, Bahir Dar, AMARA, Danakil Desert, Red Sea, DJIBOUTI, Gulf of Aden, AFAR, BINSHANGUL GUMUZ, ETHIOPIA, Ethiopian Highlands, LEKEMPTI, WELLEGA, & GIMBI, GUJI, OROMO, LIMU, ADDIS ABABA, Dire Dawa, HARAR, SOMALIA, SOUTH SUDAN, ILLUBABOR, AMARO, DJIMMAH, KAMBATA, ARSI, BALE, SUMALE, GAMBELA HIZBOCH, WELAYTA, KAFFA, Lake Abaya, YIRGACHEFFE, OROMIYA, TEPI, SOUTHERN, SIDAMO, BEBEKA, BORENA, Great Rift Valley, KENYA

KENYA

Kenya offers some of the most intensely aromatic, brightly acidic coffees in the world. Flavours from region to region vary subtly, but most feature uniquely complex fruit and berry notes, citrus acidity, and juicy, rich textures.

Only around 330 farms in Kenya are estates of 15 hectares (37 acres) or more. Just over half of the coffee producers are smallholders with only a couple of hectares of land each. These smallholders are grouped into factories that belong to cooperative societies, each factory receiving coffee cherries from hundreds, to even a couple of thousand, producers.

Kenya grows Arabica, specifically SL, K7, and Ruiru varieties. Most beans are washed for export (see pp20–21); usually any smaller selections of naturally processed coffee cherries are consumed in Kenya. Once processed, most of the coffee beans are traded via a weekly auction system, where exporters bid on samples they tasted the previous week. Although this is still susceptible to swings of the commodity market, prices at the auction reward the best-quality coffees and thus provide incentives for producers to improve agricultural practices and the quality of their coffee.

CHARACTERISTIC RED SOIL
Kenya's aluminium and iron-rich red clay soil contributes to the unique flavour of its coffee.

KENYAN COFFEE KEY FACTS

PERCENTAGE OF WORLD MARKET: LESS THAN **0.5%**

HARVEST:
MAIN CROP
OCTOBER–DECEMBER
SMALL "FLY" CROP
APRIL–JUNE

MAIN TYPES:
ARABICA
SL 28, SL 34, K7, RUIRU 11, BATIAN

PROCESSES:
WASHED, SOME NATURAL PROCESS

LOCAL TECHNIQUE
Kenyans are conducting research on a large quantity of wild Arabica trees as well as smaller numbers of eight other wild Rubiaceae species that have been found in the Marsabit forest.

WORLD RANKING AS A PRODUCER: 22ND LARGEST COFFEE PRODUCER IN THE WORLD

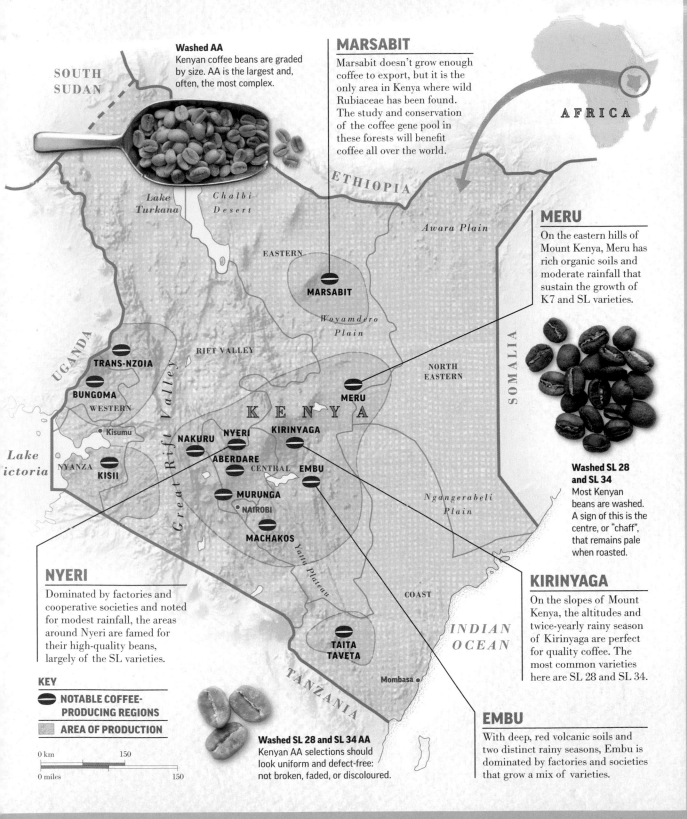

Washed AA
Kenyan coffee beans are graded by size. AA is the largest and, often, the most complex.

SOUTH SUDAN

MARSABIT

Marsabit doesn't grow enough coffee to export, but it is the only area in Kenya where wild Rubiaceae has been found. The study and conservation of the coffee gene pool in these forests will benefit coffee all over the world.

AFRICA

ETHIOPIA

Lake Turkana

Chalbi Desert

Awara Plain

EASTERN

MERU

On the eastern hills of Mount Kenya, Meru has rich organic soils and moderate rainfall that sustain the growth of K7 and SL varieties.

MARSABIT

Woyamdero Plain

SOMALIA

NORTH EASTERN

RIFT VALLEY

UGANDA

TRANS-NZOIA

BUNGOMA

WESTERN

KENYA

MERU

• Kisumu

NAKURU   NYERI   KIRINYAGA

ABERDARE

Lake Victoria

NYANZA

KISII

CENTRAL   EMBU

Washed SL 28 and SL 34
Most Kenyan beans are washed. A sign of this is the centre, or "chaff", that remains pale when roasted.

MURUNGA

• NAIROBI

Ngangerabeli Plain

MACHAKOS

Yatta Plateau

NYERI

Dominated by factories and cooperative societies and noted for modest rainfall, the areas around Nyeri are famed for their high-quality beans, largely of the SL varieties.

COAST

KIRINYAGA

On the slopes of Mount Kenya, the altitudes and twice-yearly rainy season of Kirinyaga are perfect for quality coffee. The most common varieties here are SL 28 and SL 34.

INDIAN OCEAN

KEY

⬤ **NOTABLE COFFEE-PRODUCING REGIONS**

▦ **AREA OF PRODUCTION**

0 km   150

0 miles   150

TAITA TAVETA

TANZANIA

Mombasa •

Washed SL 28 and SL 34 AA
Kenyan AA selections should look uniform and defect-free: not broken, faded, or discoloured.

EMBU

With deep, red volcanic soils and two distinct rainy seasons, Embu is dominated by factories and societies that grow a mix of varieties.

TANZANIA

Flavours of Tanzanian coffee can be split between the heavy-bodied, sweet, naturally processed Robustas and Arabicas near Lake Victoria, and the bright, citrus, berry-like washed Arabicas of the rest of the country.

Coffee was introduced to Tanzania by Catholic missionaries in 1898. Today, Tanzania grows some Robusta, but the majority of the crop is Arabica – Bourbon, Kent, Nyassa, and the famous Blue Mountain. It is prone to wild swings in production, from 534,000 bags in 2011 to over 1 million bags in 2012. Around 20 per cent of Tanzania's export earnings come from coffee. Yield of fruit per tree is low, adding to other growing challenges, such as low prices and a lack of training and equipment.

Almost all of the beans are grown by smallholders on family farms. About 450,000 families are involved in coffee growing, and the industry as a whole employs around 2.5 million people.

As with some other African countries, the coffee is sold at auction, but there is a "direct" window open for buyers who wish to buy from the exporters themselves. This window allows higher-quality coffee to be rewarded with higher prices, creating a sustainable cycle of production in the long term.

CHERRY RIPENING
Cherries ripen at different speeds. Pickers return to the same tree several times to collect ripe ones.

TANZANIAN COFFEE KEY FACTS

PERCENTAGE OF WORLD MARKET: **0.6%**

MAIN TYPES:
70% ARABICA
BOURBON, KENT, NYASSA, BLUE MOUNTAIN
30% ROBUSTA

HARVEST:
ARABICA **JULY–FEBRUARY**
ROBUSTA **APRIL–DECEMBER**

PROCESSES:
ARABICA **WASHED**
ROBUSTA **NATURAL**

WORLD RANKING AS A PRODUCER: **18TH LARGEST COFFEE PRODUCER IN THE WORLD**

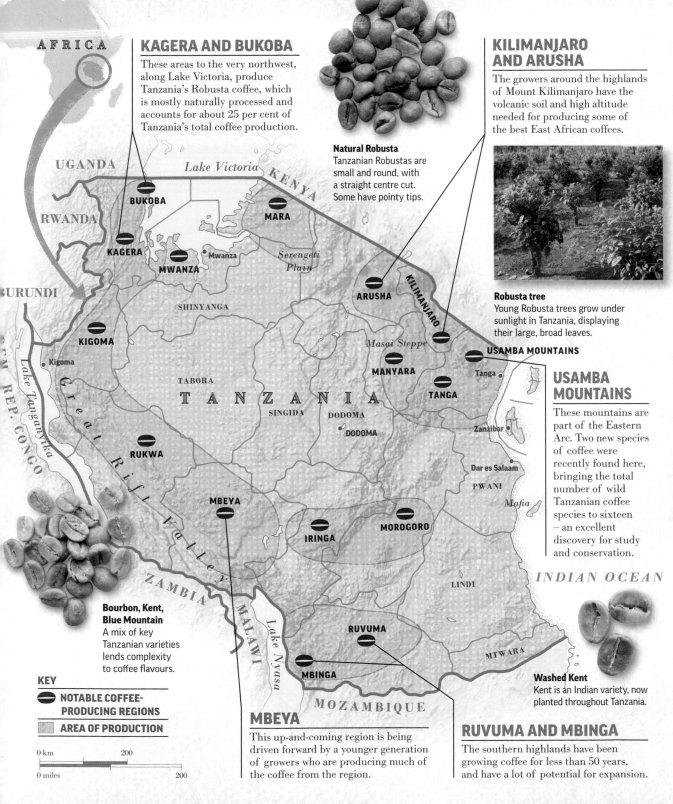

KAGERA AND BUKOBA

These areas to the very northwest, along Lake Victoria, produce Tanzania's Robusta coffee, which is mostly naturally processed and accounts for about 25 per cent of Tanzania's total coffee production.

KILIMANJARO AND ARUSHA

The growers around the highlands of Mount Kilimanjaro have the volcanic soil and high altitude needed for producing some of the best East African coffees.

Natural Robusta
Tanzanian Robustas are small and round, with a straight centre cut. Some have pointy tips.

Robusta tree
Young Robusta trees grow under sunlight in Tanzania, displaying their large, broad leaves.

USAMBA MOUNTAINS

These mountains are part of the Eastern Arc. Two new species of coffee were recently found here, bringing the total number of wild Tanzanian coffee species to sixteen – an excellent discovery for study and conservation.

Bourbon, Kent, Blue Mountain
A mix of key Tanzanian varieties lends complexity to coffee flavours.

Washed Kent
Kent is an Indian variety, now planted throughout Tanzania.

KEY
⬬ NOTABLE COFFEE-PRODUCING REGIONS
▦ AREA OF PRODUCTION

0 km   200
0 miles   200

MBEYA

This up-and-coming region is being driven forward by a younger generation of growers who are producing much of the coffee from the region.

RUVUMA AND MBINGA

The southern highlands have been growing coffee for less than 50 years, and have a lot of potential for expansion.

UGANDA · RWANDA · BURUNDI · DEM. REP. CONGO · ZAMBIA · MALAWI · MOZAMBIQUE · KENYA

Lake Victoria · KILIMANJARO · Serengeti Plain · Masai Steppe · Great Rift Valley · Lake Tanganyika · Lake Nyasa · INDIAN OCEAN

BUKOBA · KAGERA · MWANZA · Mwanza · MARA · ARUSHA · KIGOMA · Kigoma · SHINYANGA · TABORA · MANYARA · TANGA · Tanga · USAMBA MOUNTAINS · TANZANIA · SINGIDA · DODOMA · Zanzibar · Dar es Salaam · PWANI · Mafia · RUKWA · MBEYA · IRINGA · MOROGORO · LINDI · RUVUMA · MBINGA · MTWARA

RWANDA

The coffees from Rwanda are often some of the softest, sweetest, and most floral of East African coffees – delicately balanced and rapidly winning the hearts of coffee lovers worldwide.

The first coffee trees in Rwanda were planted in 1904, and export began around 1917. The high altitudes and steady rainfalls mean the potential for quality is very high.

About half of the country's export revenue now comes from the coffee industry, so coffee has recently become a vehicle for the government to improve socio-economic conditions. There has been an explosion in the number of washing stations built throughout the country, giving the 500,000 smallholdings easier access to resources and training.

One of the challenges for Rwandan coffee is the "potato" defect – a bacteria that can cause the occasional bean to smell and taste like raw potato. However, the dominance of old Bourbon trees and the combination of high altitudes and rich soil ensure that Rwandan beans are still some of the best on the market.

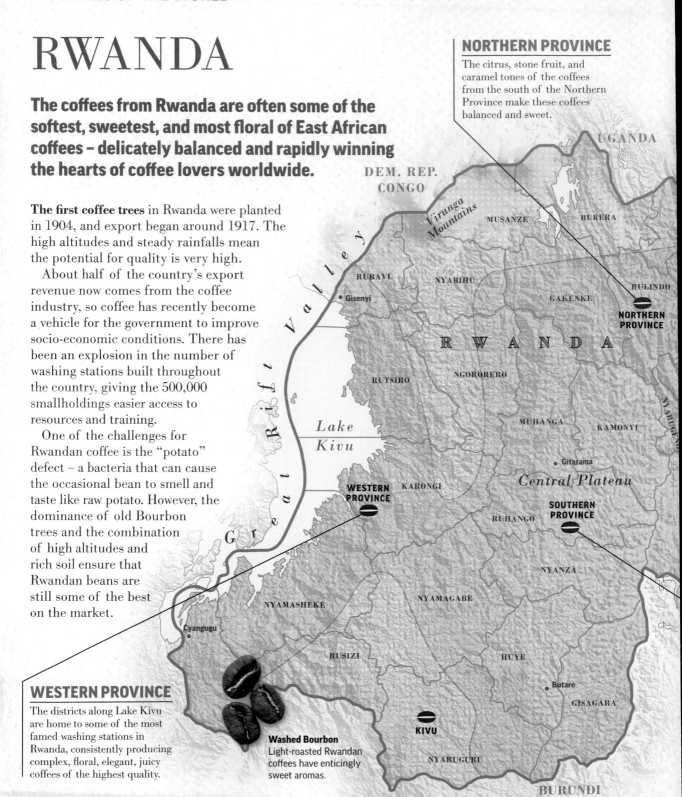

NORTHERN PROVINCE
The citrus, stone fruit, and caramel tones of the coffees from the south of the Northern Province make these coffees balanced and sweet.

WESTERN PROVINCE
The districts along Lake Kivu are home to some of the most famed washing stations in Rwanda, consistently producing complex, floral, elegant, juicy coffees of the highest quality.

Washed Bourbon
Light-roasted Rwandan coffees have enticingly sweet aromas.

AFRICA

NYAGATARE

TANZANIA

GATSIBO

*Eastern
Plain*

GICUMBI

KAYONZA

*Lake
Ihema*

EASTERN
PROVINCE

GASABO

Kabuga

CUKIRO

*Lake
Cyambwe*

RWAMAGANA

NGOMA

KIREHE

BUGESERA

*Lake
Rweru*

RWANDAN COFFEE KEY FACTS

PERCENTAGE OF WORLD MARKET: **0.2%**

HARVEST:
ARABICA
MARCH–AUGUST
ROBUSTA
MAY–JUNE

MAIN TYPES:
99% ARABICA
BOURBON, CATURRA, CATUAI
1% ROBUSTA

PROCESSES:
WASHED, SOME NATURAL

WORLD RANKING AS A PRODUCER: **32ND LARGEST PRODUCER IN THE WORLD**

Washed Catuai
Rwandan soil enhances the floral and stone-fruit flavours of varieties such as Catuai – apparent after roasting.

Unripe Arabica cherries
When these ripen, Rwandan pickers gather each cherry by hand.

EASTERN PROVINCE

The southeast corner of Rwanda is home to a small number of washing stations and farms that are slowly gaining a reputation for coffees with rich chocolate and forest-fruit notes.

SOUTHERN PROVINCE

The higher elevations of Rwanda's southern province produces coffees with classic floral or citrus flavours and delicate creamy textures – subtle and sweet.

Washed Bourbon
Rwanda has preserved most of its old Bourbon variety, highly sought after by the speciality market.

KEY

⬤ **NOTABLE COFFEE-PRODUCING REGIONS**

▨ **AREA OF PRODUCTION**

0 km   20
0 miles   20

HOME ROASTING

Roast your beans at home to get them to your preferred flavour. To do this, you can use an electric home roaster for a controlled approach, or simply heat a batch of coffee beans in a wok over your stove, stirring frequently.

HOW TO ROAST

Finding a balance between time, temperature, and overall degree of roast can take some practice, but roasting is a fascinating and satisfying route to understanding more about the potential flavours of coffee. Keeping within certain parameters, you should be able to experiment and taste until you find a method that works for your beans. There is no one-way-fits-all recipe to roasting coffee that tastes good, as well as looks brown. Keep notes on both roasting process and flavour results, and you will soon learn how to manipulate the roast as desired. Aim for an overall roasting time of 10 to 20 minutes. Shorter than this, and the coffee might be green and taste astringent. Longer than this, and it might taste flat and hollow. If you buy an electric home roaster, follow your manufacturer's instructions.

THE STAGES OF THE ROAST

Coffee beans transform as they are roasted, increasing in size, smoothening, and eliciting a range of aromas.

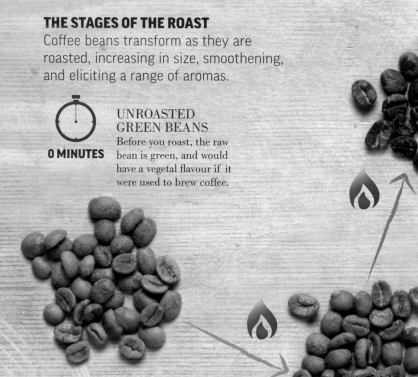

0 MINUTES

UNROASTED GREEN BEANS
Before you roast, the raw bean is green, and would have a vegetal flavour if it were used to brew coffee.

6 MINUTES

HIGH PRESSURE
As the water in the bean heats up, steam pressure builds up within the structure and the colour continues to deepen. Some beans turn a shade of brown that makes them look nearly done, but they should briefly pale a little once they reach the next vital stage of the roast, the first crack.

3 MINUTES

DRYING PHASE
The beginning of roasting is called the drying phase. Here, the bean turns from green through yellow, to light brown. This phase allows water to evaporate and acids to react and break down, removing the vegetal taste of the bean. The bean smells like popcorn or toast, and the colour changes can make it look "wrinkled".

GREEN COFFEE BEANS

If you start with fresh, high-quality green beans – readily available online or in specialist coffee shops – you'll soon be able to create home-roasted coffee to rival anything you would find on the high street. You need to be prepared to try again and again – there is a high chance that you may ruin the flavour of the coffee beans, even if they are of the best quality.

There is no way to take old or low-quality green coffee and make it taste great. All you can do is roast the beans so dark that you cover up the flat, wooden, baggy taste with burnt flavours.

TIP
Once you are happy with the roast, cool the beans down for 2–4 minutes and give them a day or two to de-gas before you use them. If you are brewing espresso, allow more time – about 1 week – for this stage.

13 MINUTES

ROASTING PHASE
Sugars, acids, and compounds react, developing flavours. Acids break down, the sugars caramelize, and the cell structure dries out and weakens.

9 MINUTES

FIRST CRACK
The force of the steam eventually causes the cell structure to rupture, making a sound a bit like popcorn popping. This is where the bean increases in size, gains a smoother surface and an even colour, and starts to smell like coffee. Stop the roast 1–2 minutes after the first crack for filter or French press brewing.

16 MINUTES

SECOND CRACK
Eventually you reach a second crack, caused by gas pressure, and oils will be forced to the surface of the brittle bean. Many espressos are roasted to the beginning or middle of the second crack.

20 MINUTES

BEYOND SECOND CRACK
You have little left of the original flavour of the coffee in the bean. It will mostly be dominated by roasty, ashy, and bitter tastes. As oils travel to the surface, they also oxidize and become harsh-tasting quite quickly.

BURUNDI

Producing coffees that range from soft, floral, and sweetly citrus to chocolatey and nutty, Burundi offers few distinct regional flavour profiles, but its diverse coffees capture interest from speciality companies.

Burundi has been growing coffee only since the 1930s, and it has taken a while for its great coffees to get onto the radar of connoisseurs. The coffee sector has struggled through political instability and climatic challenges, and being a landlocked country makes it difficult to get coffee to buyers without quality suffering noticeably.

Robusta grows in some small pockets, but the majority of the crop is Arabica – washed Bourbon, Jackson, or Mibirizi, grown largely

organic as funds for chemical fertilizers or pesticides have not been available. There are about 600,000 smallholders with 200–300 trees each, who normally also grow other food crops or keep livestock. Growers deliver to washing stations (see Local Technique below). These stations are members of Sogestals – managing firms who look after the transport and commercial aspects.

Coffee suffers from the potato defect (see p64), but local research aims to reduce the problem.

BOURBON CHERRIES
Burundi grows mostly Bourbon, which was introduced to Réunion Island by French missionaries.

BURUNDIAN COFFEE KEY FACTS

PERCENTAGE OF WORLD MARKET: LESS THAN **0.5%**

HARVEST: FEBRUARY–JUNE

MAIN TYPES:
96% ARABICA
BOURBON, JACKSON, MIBIRIZI
4% ROBUSTA

PROCESS: WASHED

WORLD RANKING AS A PRODUCER: 31ST LARGEST COFFEE PRODUCER IN THE WORLD

LOCAL TECHNIQUE
There are over 160 washing stations dotted around the hilly areas of Burundi. These stations wash the coffee beans in specialized tanks (see p21).

Washed Bourbon
Bourbon trees have been left
undisturbed here for decades.

KAYANZA

The Kayanza region is located
in the north of Burundi, which
is close to the border with
Rwanda. Coffee beans from
here are traditionally of
very good quality.

Lake
Riveru

AFRICA

**Washed
Bourbon**
Sweet and
citrus, Burundi
Bourbon is most
aromatic in
light roasts.

RWANDA

KIRUNDO

CIBITOKE

MUYINGA

Muyinga

NGOZI

DEM. REP.
CONGO

KAYANZA

BUBANZA

KARUZI

CANKUZO

MURAMVYA

KIRIMIRO

MUMIRWA

BUJUMBURA

B U R U N D I

BUJUMBURA

MWARO

GITEGA

RUYIGI

Flowering Arabica
Coffee trees flower in Burundi
between June and August.

Lake Tanganyika

BURURI

RUTANA

MUMIRWA

This Sogestal lies
in the west, in the
mountains of
Kumugaruro,
southwest of Kibira
National Park.
The high altitudes
provide perfect
conditions for
growing coffee.

MAKAMBA

KEY

⬤ **NOTABLE COFFEE-
PRODUCING REGIONS**

▨ **AREA OF PRODUCTION**

0 km   30

0 miles   30

KIRIMIRO

Close to Gitega in the
centre of the country,
the areas covered by this
Sogestal have washing
stations at the highest
altitude in Burundi.

UGANDA

Robusta is indigenous to Uganda, and still grows wild in some places – little wonder that the country is the world's second largest exporter of Robusta coffee.

Arabica was introduced in the early 1900s, and most of it is now grown on the foothills of Mount Elgon. About 3 million families rely on the coffee sector for income. Some Arabica is produced, including Typica and SL varieties.

For both Arabica and Robusta, new production and processing practices increase coffee quality. Robusta, generally thought of as inferior to Arabica and traditionally grown in lowland areas, grows here at heights of 1,500m (4,900ft). The beans are also washed, not naturally processed (see pp20–21). As quality improves, farmers reap the rewards of good agricultural practice.

Natural Robusta
Ugandans call washed coffees "wugars", and naturally processed coffees "drugars".

AFRICA

BUGISU

The small farms of Bugisu and Mount Elgon sit 1,600–1,900m (5,250–6,200ft) above sea level, and produce washed Arabicas with heavy textures and sweet and chocolatey flavours.

Nangeya Mountains

DEM. REP. CONGO

WEST NILE

Lake Albert

Gulu

NORTHERN

NORTHERN REGION

Lira

U G A N D A

Great Rift Valley

Lake Kyoga

WESTERN REGION

WESTERN

Mbale

EASTERN

BUGISU

KENYA

CENTRAL & SOUTHWEST

Mukono

Jinja

KAMPALA

Kasese

LAKE VICTORIA BASIN

Lake Edward

Masaka

Lake Victoria

Mbarara

TANZANIA

WESTERN REGION

Snow-capped Mount Rwenzori in the west is home to the naturally processed Arabicas of Uganda, known as "Drugars". Coffees can be wine-like with fruity notes and good acidity.

LAKE VICTORIA BASIN

Robusta grows well in loamy, clay-rich soils, so the area around the Lake Victoria Basin is well suited. It also benefits from the high altitudes, increasing acidity and adding complexity.

UGANDAN COFFEE KEY FACTS

PERCENTAGE OF WORLD MARKET: **2%**

MAIN TYPES:
80% ROBUSTA
20% ARABICA
TYPICA, SL 14, SL 28, KENT

HARVESTS:
ARABICA
OCTOBER–FEBRUARY
ROBUSTA
ALL YEAR, PEAK IN NOVEMBER–FEBRUARY

PROCESSES:
WASHED AND **NATURAL**

WORLD RANKING AS A PRODUCER: **11TH LARGEST PRODUCER IN THE WORLD**

KEY

● NOTABLE COFFEE-PRODUCING REGIONS

▨ AREA OF PRODUCTION

0 km 100

0 miles 100

MALAWI

One of the world's smallest producers, Malawi is drawing interest for its subtle, floral, East African coffees.

Coffee came to Malawi in 1891, brought by the British. Uniquely, the Arabica varieties here are predominantly Geisha and Catimor, with some Agaro, Mundo Novo, Bourbon, and Blue Mountain. Kenyan SL 28 is also being planted to help to invigorate the speciality sector.

Unlike other African countries, many coffee trees are grown on terraces to try to combat soil erosion and retain water. Malawi produces about 20,000 bags on average per year, and consumes very few of those internally. About 500,000 smallholders grow coffee.

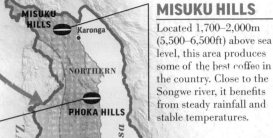

MISUKU HILLS

Located 1,700–2,000m (5,500–6,500ft) above sea level, this area produces some of the best coffee in the country. Close to the Songwe river, it benefits from steady rainfall and stable temperatures.

PHOKA HILLS

In Livingstonia, between the Nyika National Park plateau and Chilamba Bay, coffee grows on the Phoka hills at altitudes of about 1,700m (5,500ft) above sea level. It produces sweet, subtly floral, and elegant coffees.

NKHATA BAY HIGHLANDS

To the southeast and southwest of Mzuzu, the Nkhata Bay Highlands stretch up to 2,000m (6,500ft) above sea level, and have a hot and rainy climate. Some coffees taste very similar to those from Ethiopia.

Washed Catimor
At high altitudes in Malawi, Catimors gain a pleasing acidity, which comes through when roasted.

Washed Bourbon, Geisha, Agaro
The range of varieties in Malawi attracts interest from speciality companies.

KEY
- NOTABLE COFFEE-PRODUCING REGIONS
- AREA OF PRODUCTION

MALAWIAN COFFEE KEY FACTS

PERCENTAGE OF WORLD MARKET: 0.01%

HARVEST: JUNE–OCTOBER

PROCESS: WASHED

MAIN TYPES: ARABICA AGARO, GEISHA, CATIMOR, MUNDO NOVO, BOURBON, BLUE MOUNTAIN, CATURRA

WORLD RANKING AS A PRODUCER: 43RD LARGEST PRODUCER IN THE WORLD

COFFEES OF THE WORLD
INDONESIA, ASIA, AND OCEANIA

INDIA

Indian Arabica and Robusta are especially popular for espresso preparation, because they are heavy-bodied and low in acidity. There are some defined regional flavour attributes, and exporters are keen to discover more.

Coffee in India is grown under shade, normally alongside other crops, such as pepper, cardamom, ginger, nuts, oranges, vanilla, bananas, mangoes, and jackfruits. At harvest, coffee cherries are either washed, naturally processed, or "monsooned" (see Local Technique, below) – a method that is unique to India.

Arabica grows here, including Catimor, Kent, and S 795 varieties, but the majority of the crop is Robusta. There are about 250,000 growers in India, nearly all of whom are smallholders. For almost a million people, coffee is a livelihood. Harvest takes place twice a year for Robusta, but this often varies by several weeks depending on the climatic conditions.

In the last five years, production has averaged at just under 5 million bags per year. Around 80 per cent of this is exported, but more and more Indians choose to drink local coffee.

Traditional Indian filter coffee, made from three-quarters coffee and one quarter chicory, is popular around the country.

ROBUSTA CHERRIES
After harvest, Indian Robusta beans are sometimes processed using the monsooned method.

INDIAN COFFEE KEY FACTS

PERCENTAGE OF WORLD MARKET: **3.5%**

MAIN TYPES:
60% ROBUSTA
40% ARABICA
CAUVERY/CATIMOR, KENT, S 795, SELECTIONS 4, 5B, 9, 10, SAN RAMON, CATURRA, DEVAMACHY

HARVEST:
ARABICA
OCTOBER–FEBRUARY
ROBUSTA
JANUARY–MARCH

PROCESSES:
NATURAL, WASHED, SEMI-WASHED, AND **MONSOONED**

LOCAL TECHNIQUE
The unique monsooned processing method exposes coffee cherries to hot, humid weather and wind, making them swell, fade, and change in flavour.

WORLD RANKING AS A PRODUCER: 6TH LARGEST COFFEE PRODUCER IN THE WORLD

ASIA

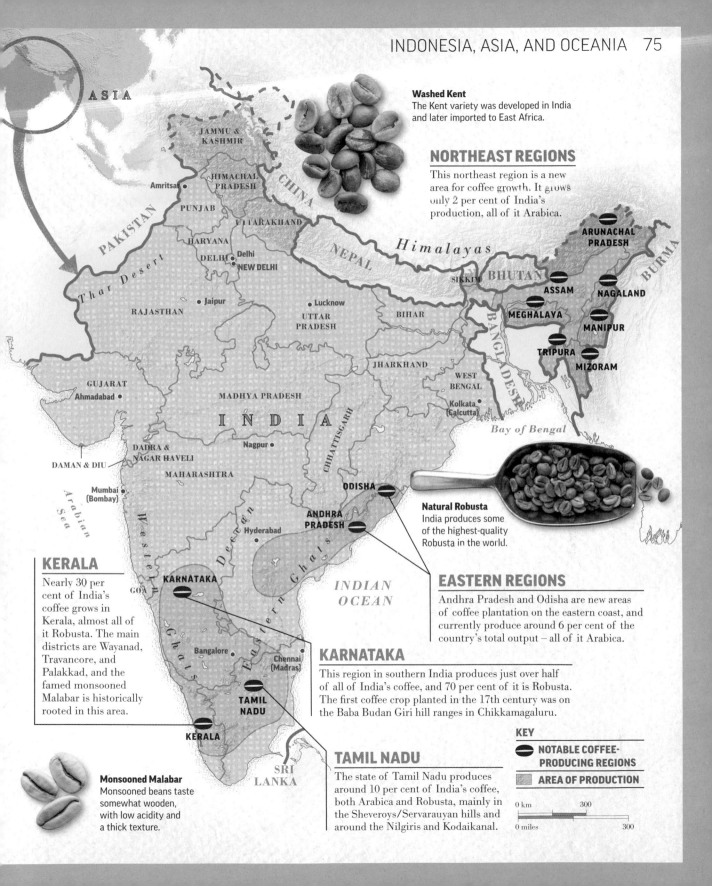

Washed Kent
The Kent variety was developed in India and later imported to East Africa.

NORTHEAST REGIONS

This northeast region is a new area for coffee growth. It grows only 2 per cent of India's production, all of it Arabica.

Natural Robusta
India produces some of the highest-quality Robusta in the world.

KERALA

Nearly 30 per cent of India's coffee grows in Kerala, almost all of it Robusta. The main districts are Wayanad, Travancore, and Palakkad, and the famed monsooned Malabar is historically rooted in this area.

EASTERN REGIONS

Andhra Pradesh and Odisha are new areas of coffee plantation on the eastern coast, and currently produce around 6 per cent of the country's total output – all of it Arabica.

KARNATAKA

This region in southern India produces just over half of all of India's coffee, and 70 per cent of it is Robusta. The first coffee crop planted in the 17th century was on the Baba Budan Giri hill ranges in Chikkamagaluru.

TAMIL NADU

The state of Tamil Nadu produces around 10 per cent of India's coffee, both Arabica and Robusta, mainly in the Sheveroys/Servarauyan hills and around the Nilgiris and Kodaikanal.

Monsooned Malabar
Monsooned beans taste somewhat wooden, with low acidity and a thick texture.

KEY

⬤ **NOTABLE COFFEE-PRODUCING REGIONS**

▨ **AREA OF PRODUCTION**

0 km   300

0 miles   300

SUMATRA

Sumatra is the largest island within Indonesia. Coffees here can have wooden notes, heavy textures, low acidity, and flavours that range from earthy, cedary, and spicy, to fermented fruit, cocoa, herbs, leather, and tobacco.

Indonesia produces mostly rustic-flavoured Robusta and a small proportion of Arabica. The first coffee plantations in Sumatra appeared in 1888, and they are now the largest producer of Indonesian Robusta, supplying around 75 per cent of the country's total output.

Of the Arabicas, Typica is still the most common. Some Bourbon, as well as S-line hybrids, Caturra, Catimor, Hibrido de Timor (Tim Tim), and Ethiopian lines called Rambung and Abyssinia are also grown here. Producers often grow mixed plots of various trees, causing a lot of natural hybridization. Water can be scarce, so smallholders mostly use the traditional Giling Basah processing method (see Local Technique below), giving the coffee its blue-green colour. Unfortunately, the method can cause damaged beans and defect taints.

The quality of Indonesian coffees is inconsistent, and internal logistical challenges make it difficult to source premium selections.

RIPE ROBUSTA FRUIT
Sumatran Robusta trees grow predominantly in the central and southern part of the island.

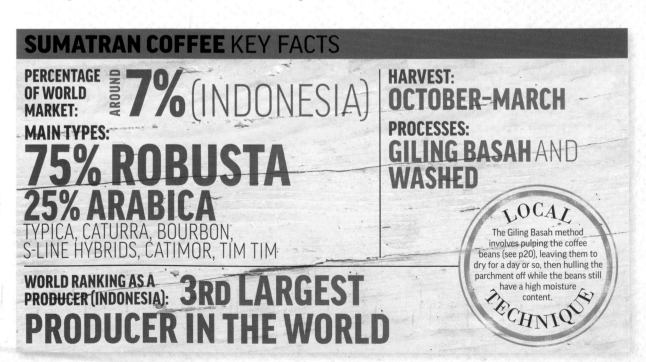

SUMATRAN COFFEE KEY FACTS

PERCENTAGE OF WORLD MARKET: AROUND **7%** (INDONESIA)

MAIN TYPES:
75% ROBUSTA
25% ARABICA
TYPICA, CATURRA, BOURBON, S-LINE HYBRIDS, CATIMOR, TIM TIM

WORLD RANKING AS A PRODUCER (INDONESIA): 3RD LARGEST PRODUCER IN THE WORLD

HARVEST:
OCTOBER–MARCH

PROCESSES:
GILING BASAH AND **WASHED**

LOCAL TECHNIQUE
The Giling Basah method involves pulping the coffee beans (see p20), leaving them to dry for a day or so, then hulling the parchment off while the beans still have a high moisture content.

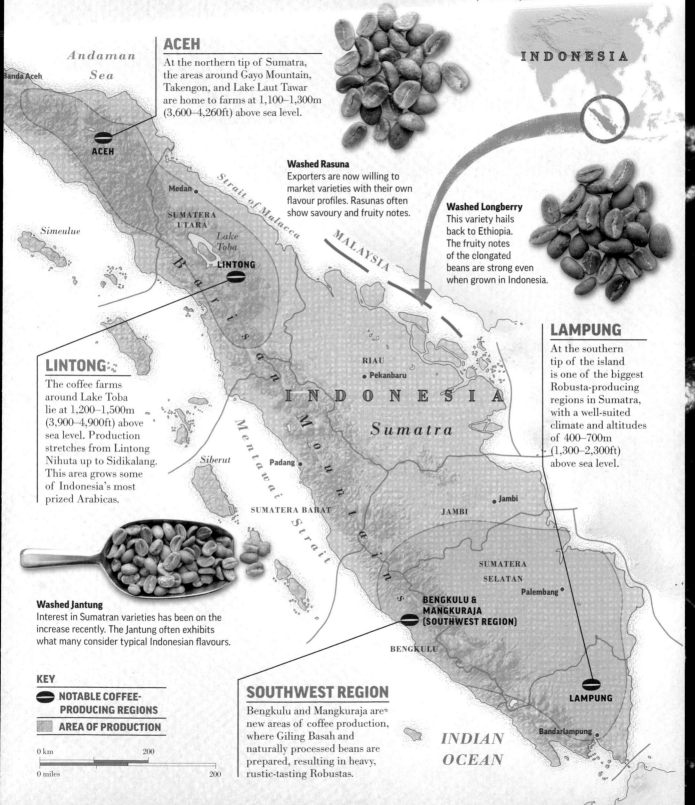

INDONESIA

ACEH

At the northern tip of Sumatra, the areas around Gayo Mountain, Takengon, and Lake Laut Tawar are home to farms at 1,100–1,300m (3,600–4,260ft) above sea level.

Washed Rasuna
Exporters are now willing to market varieties with their own flavour profiles. Rasunas often show savoury and fruity notes.

Washed Longberry
This variety hails back to Ethiopia. The fruity notes of the elongated beans are strong even when grown in Indonesia.

LINTONG

The coffee farms around Lake Toba lie at 1,200–1,500m (3,900–4,900ft) above sea level. Production stretches from Lintong Nihuta up to Sidikalang. This area grows some of Indonesia's most prized Arabicas.

LAMPUNG

At the southern tip of the island is one of the biggest Robusta-producing regions in Sumatra, with a well-suited climate and altitudes of 400–700m (1,300–2,300ft) above sea level.

Washed Jantung
Interest in Sumatran varieties has been on the increase recently. The Jantung often exhibits what many consider typical Indonesian flavours.

SOUTHWEST REGION

Bengkulu and Mangkuraja are new areas of coffee production, where Giling Basah and naturally processed beans are prepared, resulting in heavy, rustic-tasting Robustas.

KEY

⬤ **NOTABLE COFFEE-PRODUCING REGIONS**

▨ **AREA OF PRODUCTION**

0 km   200

0 miles   200

Andaman Sea

Banda Aceh

ACEH

Medan

SUMATERA UTARA

Lake Toba

LINTONG

Simeulue

Strait of Malacca

Barisan

MALAYSIA

RIAU

Pekanbaru

I N D O N E S I A

Sumatra

Mentawai Strait

Siberut

Padang

SUMATERA BARAT

Mountains

JAMBI

Jambi

SUMATERA SELATAN

Palembang

BENGKULU & MANGKURAJA (SOUTHWEST REGION)

BENGKULU

LAMPUNG

Bandarlampung

INDIAN OCEAN

SULAWESI

Of all the islands in Indonesia, Sulawesi grows the most Arabica trees. Well-processed coffees display flavours of grapefruit, berries, nuts, and spices. Coffees often taste savoury, and most have low acidity and thick texture.

Sulawesi represents only about 2 per cent of Indonesia's coffee crop, with roughly 7,000 tonnes of Arabica produced per year. Some Robusta is also grown, but it is largely consumed in Sulawesi, rather than being exported.

Sulawesi has iron-rich soils and grows old Typica, S 795, and Jember varieties at very high altitudes. Most of the farmers here are smallholders – only about 5 per cent of the crop comes from larger estates. Giling Basah is the traditional processing method, as used in Sumatra (see p76). This results in coffee beans that display a hint of the classic Indonesian dark-green colour.

Some producers are starting to wash coffee beans (see pp20–21) in a similar way to Central America, which helps to add value to their product. Much of this development is due to Japanese importers, who are the biggest buyers and have invested heavily in the Sulawesian coffee industry to ensure high-quality standards are met.

RIPENING ROBUSTA
The small proportion of Robusta trees in Sulawesi are mostly found in the northeastern areas.

SULAWESIAN COFFEE KEY FACTS

PERCENTAGE OF WORLD MARKET: AROUND **7%** (INDONESIA)

HARVEST: JULY–SEPTEMBER

MAIN TYPES: 95% ARABICA TYPICA, S 795, JEMBER **5% ROBUSTA**

PROCESSES: GILING BASAH AND WASHED

WORLD RANKING AS A PRODUCER (INDONESIA): 3RD LARGEST COFFEE PRODUCER IN THE WORLD

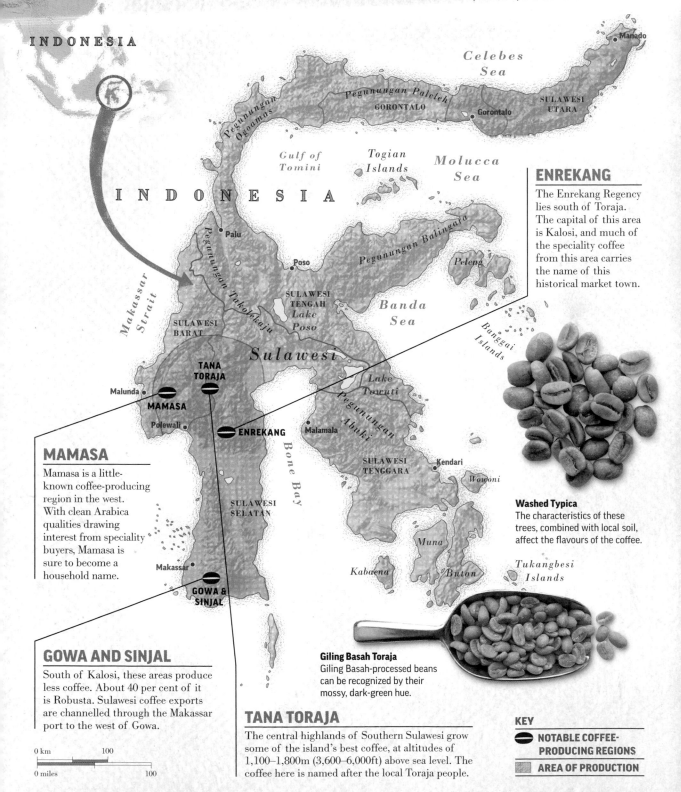

INDONESIA

I N D O N E S I A

Celebes Sea

Manado

Pegunungan Paleleh
GORONTALO
SULAWESI
UTARA
Gorontalo

Pegunungan Ogoamas

Gulf of Tomini

Togian Islands

Molucca Sea

Palu

Poso

Pegunungan Balingara

Peleng

SULAWESI
TENGAH
Lake Poso

Banda Sea

Banggai Islands

Makassar Strait

SULAWESI
BARAT

Pegunungan Takolekaju

Sulawesi

TANA
TORAJA

Malunda

MAMASA

Polewali

ENREKANG

Malamala

Lake Towuti

Pegunungan Abuki

SULAWESI
TENGGARA

Kendari

Wowoni

SULAWESI
SELATAN

Bone Bay

Makassar

GOWA &
SINJAL

Muna

Buton

Kabaena

Tukangbesi Islands

ENREKANG

The Enrekang Regency lies south of Toraja. The capital of this area is Kalosi, and much of the speciality coffee from this area carries the name of this historical market town.

Washed Typica
The characteristics of these trees, combined with local soil, affect the flavours of the coffee.

MAMASA

Mamasa is a little-known coffee-producing region in the west. With clean Arabica qualities drawing interest from speciality buyers, Mamasa is sure to become a household name.

Giling Basah Toraja
Giling Basah-processed beans can be recognized by their mossy, dark-green hue.

GOWA AND SINJAL

South of Kalosi, these areas produce less coffee. About 40 per cent of it is Robusta. Sulawesi coffee exports are channelled through the Makassar port to the west of Gowa.

0 km   100

0 miles   100

TANA TORAJA

The central highlands of Southern Sulawesi grow some of the island's best coffee, at altitudes of 1,100–1,800m (3,600–6,000ft) above sea level. The coffee here is named after the local Toraja people.

KEY

⬤ NOTABLE COFFEE-
PRODUCING REGIONS

▨ AREA OF PRODUCTION

JAVA

The island of Java offers few regional flavour profiles, but in general, coffees are low in acidity, nutty or earthy, and heavy-bodied. Some are aged for a rustic flavour.

INDONESIA

WEST HIGHLANDS

New private plantings are taking place in Western Java. Experimental varieties such as Andung Sari, Sigararuntang, Kartika, and S-lines as well as Ateng, Jember, and very old Typica varieties grow here, and promise some exciting new beans.

Sunda Strait

Panaitan Island

Serang

JAKARTA

Tangerang

JAKARTA RAYA

BANTEN

Bogor

Lake Jatiluhur

Cirebon

Java Sea

Cianjur

WEST HIGHLANDS

Bandung

Brebes

Tegal

Pekalongan

Sukabumi

JAWA BARAT

Garut

INDONESIA

JAWA TENGAH

Ciamis

Java

CENTRAL HIGHLAND

Cilacap

Washed Arabica
Javanese Arabicas are often large and smooth, with little or no silverskin on the surface.

JAVANESE COFFEE KEY FACTS

PERCENTAGE OF WORLD MARKET: AROUND **7%** (INDONESIA)

HARVEST: JUNE–OCTOBER

PROCESS: WASHED

MAIN TYPES:
90% ROBUSTA
10% ARABICA
ANDUNG SARI, S-LINES, KARTIKA, ATENG, SIGARARUNTANG, JEMBER, TYPICA

LOCAL TECHNIQUE
Javans mainly use the washed method. This decreases the risk of taints or defects caused when the beans are processed using the Giling Basah method (see p76).

WORLD RANKING AS A PRODUCER (INDONESIA): **3RD LARGEST PRODUCER IN THE WORLD**

Indonesia was the first non-African country to cultivate coffee on a large scale. It began in 1696 with the areas around Jakarta, West Java. The first seedlings did not survive due to a flood, but in a second attempt three years later, they took root.

Production flourished until leaf rust killed most Typica trees in 1876, causing widespread planting of Robusta. New Arabica plantings did not occur until the 1950s, and still only represent about 10 per cent of Javanese coffee.

Most of the coffee grown in Java today is Robusta, but it also grows some varieties of Arabica, such as Ateng, Jember, and Typica. Coffee is largely grown on government-owned (PTP) plantations, centred at the Ijen Plateau in Eastern Java. These state-owned plantations produce washed coffees, cleaner than many other Indonesian coffees. New private plantings are taking place in Western Java, around Mount Pangalengan, making this area one to watch for the future.

ROBUSTA CLUSTER
Coffee cherries mature at different speeds – one of the reasons for the long harvest period in Java.

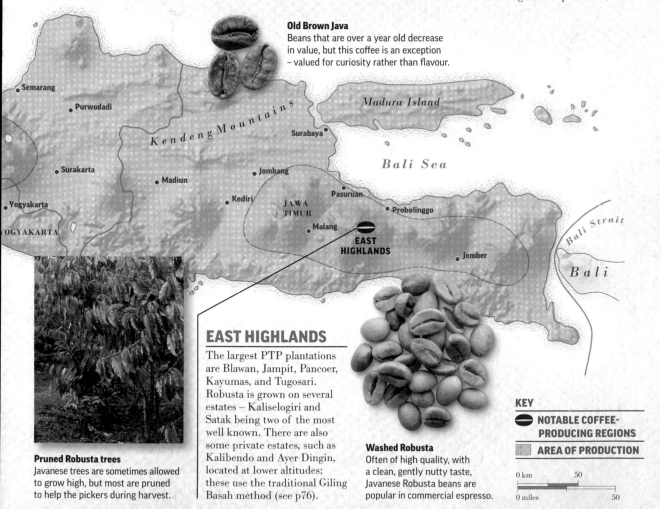

Old Brown Java
Beans that are over a year old decrease in value, but this coffee is an exception – valued for curiosity rather than flavour.

Semarang

Purwodadi

Kendeng Mountains

Surakarta

Madiun

Kediri

Yogyakarta

YOGYAKARTA

Jombang

JAWA TIMUR

Malang

EAST HIGHLANDS

Madura Island

Surabaya

Bali Sea

Pasuruan

Probolinggo

Jember

Bali Strait

Bali

Pruned Robusta trees
Javanese trees are sometimes allowed to grow high, but most are pruned to help the pickers during harvest.

EAST HIGHLANDS

The largest PTP plantations are Blawan, Jampit, Pancoer, Kayumas, and Tugosari. Robusta is grown on several estates – Kaliselogiri and Satak being two of the most well known. There are also some private estates, such as Kalibendo and Ayer Dingin, located at lower altitudes; these use the traditional Giling Basah method (see p76).

Washed Robusta
Often of high quality, with a clean, gently nutty taste, Javanese Robusta beans are popular in commercial espresso.

KEY

⬤ NOTABLE COFFEE-PRODUCING REGIONS

▦ AREA OF PRODUCTION

0 km   50

0 miles   50

COFFEE Q&A

There are many mixed messages about coffee in the media, and it can be difficult to find information that relates to you – especially as caffeine affects us all in different ways. Here are reliable answers to common coffee queries.

HOW ADDICTIVE IS COFFEE?

Coffee is not considered a drug of dependence and any "withdrawal symptoms" can be alleviated by gently decreasing the daily consumption of coffee over a short period of time.

IS COFFEE DEHYDRATING?

While coffee can have a diuretic effect, a cup of it consists of about 98 per cent water and as such is not dehydrating. Any loss of fluid is effectively offset by the intake itself.

98% WATER

CAN DRINKING COFFEE BE GOOD FOR OUR HEALTH?

Coffee and its antioxidants – caffeine and other organic compounds – have been shown to have positive effects on a wide range of health problems.

CAN COFFEE IMPROVE LEVELS OF CONCENTRATION?

Brain activity that controls concentration and memory is boosted temporarily when we drink coffee.

HOW DOES CAFFEINE KEEP US AWAKE?

Caffeine blocks a chemical called adenosine from attaching to its receptors, which would normally make you feel sleepy. The blockage also triggers the production of adrenaline, increasing your feeling of alertness.

WHAT EFFECT DOES CAFFEINE HAVE ON SPORTING ABILITY?

The effects of moderate caffeine intake can improve endurance in aerobic sports as well as performance in anaerobic exercises. It opens up your bronchial tubes, improving breathing, and releases sugar into your blood stream, directing it to muscles.

DO DARK ROASTS CONTAIN MORE CAFFEINE?

Very dark roasts might actually contain less caffeine, and definitely won't perk you up faster.

WHY DON'T I GET A CAFFEINE KICK?

You can desensitize yourself to the effects of caffeine by drinking coffee at the same time every day, so change your routine every now and then.

PAPUA NEW GUINEA

Coffees produced in Papua New Guinea have dense textures, low-to-medium acidity, and a range of herbal, wooden, and tropical- or tobacco-like flavours.

Most coffee is grown in smallholder gardens, some in plantations, and a small percentage using a state scheme. Almost all the coffee is highland-grown washed Arabica, including Bourbon, Arusha, and Mundo Novo varieties. Two to three million people rely on coffee for their livelihoods.

There is great interest for all the coffee-growing provinces to plant more trees and produce coffee of better quality.

OCEANIA

EASTERN HIGHLANDS

With high altitudes that reach 1,500–1,900m (4,900–6,200ft) above sea level and the most rain, some of the best, most complex coffees are found here.

Washed Mundo Novo Peaberry
These Peaberries (see p16) have a wine-like, juicy character.

KEY

NOTABLE COFFEE-PRODUCING REGIONS

AREA OF PRODUCTION

0 km   150
0 miles   150

Vanimo
SANDAUN
Wewak
EAST SEPIK
Central Range
MADANG
Karkar
Madang
ENGA & WESTERN HIGHLANDS
Goroka
New Guinea
CHIMBU
MOROBE
SOUTHERN HIGHLANDS
EASTERN HIGHLANDS
Lae
Lake Murray
GULF
JIWAKA
Bismarck Sea
WEST NEW BRITAIN
Vitiaz Strait
Kimbe
New Britain
EAST NEW BRITAIN
New Ireland
NEW IRELAND
Rabaul
NORTH SOLOMONS
Solomon Islands
Bougainville Island
Arawa
Solomon Sea
PAPUA NEW GUINEA
WESTERN
Gulf of Papua
NORTHERN
Popondetta
Owen Stanley Range
Kiriwina
D'Entrecasteaux Islands
PORT MORESBY
CENTRAL
MILNE BAY
Alotau
Coral sea

Washed Typica Bourbon
The Typica variety was one of the first to grow in Papua New Guinea.

ENGA AND WESTERN HIGHLANDS

These relatively dry highlands, between 1,200 and 1,800m (3,900 and 6,000ft) above sea level, grow lower-acidity beans with herbal, nutty notes.

CHIMBU AND JIWAKA

With some of the highest-grown coffee in Papua New Guinea at 1,600–1,900m (5,250–6,200ft) above sea level, the best coffees are bright, with gentle fruity notes.

PNG COFFEE

PERCENTAGE OF WORLD MARKET: LESS THAN **0.7%**

MAIN TYPES:
95% ARABICA
OLD STRAINS OF TYPICA, BOURBON, ARUSHA, BLUE MOUNTAIN, MUNDO NOVO
5% ROBUSTA

HARVEST: APRIL–SEPTEMBER

WORLD RANKING AS A PRODUCER: **17TH**

AUSTRALIA

The flavour of Australian Arabicas is varied, but often nutty, chocolatey, and softly acidic, with scope for sweetly citrus and fruity notes.

Arabica has grown here for 200 years, but the industry has gone through highs and lows. With the move to mechanical harvesting in the last 30 years, new farms have been established to revive the sector, with some producers also starting to plant on Norfolk Island, off the east coast.

Growers here plant new varieties, such as the popular K7, Catuai, and Mundo Novo, alongside old Typica and Bourbon.

AUSTRALIAN COFFEE

PERCENTAGE OF WORLD MARKET: LESS THAN **0.01%**	**HARVEST:** JUNE– OCTOBER
MAIN TYPES: **ARABICA** K7, CATUAI, MUNDO NOVO, TYPICA, BOURBON	**PROCESSES:** WASHED, PULPED, NATURAL

WORLD RANKING AS A PRODUCER: 50TH

THE ATHERTON HIGHLANDS

This region in far north Queensland produces about half of Australia's output. Most of the country's big farms can be found here. Coffees from here are often sweet, chocolatey, and nutty.

CENTRAL AND SOUTHWEST QUEENSLAND

A smaller area, there are a mix of a few small growers and some large commercial operations here. Coffees tend to be mild, sweet, and low in acidity.

Washed Catuai
Australia sources varieties, such as Catuai, that suit the climate.

Natural Bourbon
Natural processing suits areas in east Queensland with defined dry seasons.

NORTHERN NEW SOUTH WALES

With colder weather and higher altitudes, the coffee cherries ripen slower. This intensifies flavours and, potentially, lowers caffeine levels.

KEY

⬤ **NOTABLE COFFEE-PRODUCING REGIONS**

▨ **AREA OF PRODUCTION**

Arafura Sea
Darwin
Arnhem Land
Gulf of Carpentaria
Cape York Peninsula
Barkly Tableland
NORTHERN TERRITORY
Kimberley Plateau
Cairns
THE ATHERTON HIGHLANDS
Townsville
Great Sandy Desert
A U S T R A L I A
Great Dividing Range
Gibson Desert
Alice Springs
Simpson Desert
QUEENSLAND
CENTRAL & SOUTHWEST QUEENSLAND
Rockhampton
WESTERN AUSTRALIA
Great Victoria Desert
Lake Eyre North
SOUTH AUSTRALIA
Nullarbor Plain
Lake Torrens
Flinders Ranges
Brisbane
NORTHERN NEW SOUTH WALES
Perth
Darling Range
Great Australian Bight
Adelaide
NEW SOUTH WALES
Sydney
CANBERRA
AUSTRALIAN CAPITAL TERRITORY
Great Dividing Range
VICTORIA
Melbourne
Bass Strait
TASMANIA
Hobart

0 km   600
0 miles   600

THAILAND

Robustas dominate in Thailand, but the best Arabicas show soft textures, low acidity, and the potential for pleasant floral notes.

Almost all of the coffee growing in Thailand is Robusta. Most of it is naturally processed and used to make instant coffee. In the 1970s, seeing the potential for higher-quality Arabicas, farmers were encouraged to plant trees, such as Caturra, Catuai, and Catimor. Unfortunately, the follow-up on this was lacking, and farmers had little incentive to do anything with the trees. Interest in Thai coffee has grown in recent years, and investment helps farmers to produce high-quality coffee.

NORTH

The small quantity of Arabica here grows in the northern regions, at altitudes of 800–1,500m (2,620–4,900ft) above sea level. Arabicas are generally washed to optimize the premium prices they fetch over Robusta.

MYANMAR (BURMA)

SOUTHEAST ASIA

CHIANG RAI

MAE HONG SON

Chiang Mai

CHIANG MAI

LAMPANG

Tane Range

TAK

Phitsanulok

Udon Thani

Nakhon Sawan

T H A I L A N D

Bilauktaung Range

BANGKOK

Isthmus of Kra

CHUMPHON

RANONG

SURAT THANI

PHANG NA

Nakhon Si Thammarat

KRABI

NAKON SI THAMMARAT

Songkhla

Naturally processed cherries
Underripe, ripe, and overripe coffee cherries are often picked in one pass in Thailand.

Washed Arabica Peaberries
Peaberry selections (see p16) are sometimes separated out and sold on their own, particularly in northern areas.

SOUTH

Robusta grows well in the southern regions, representing nearly all the coffee grown in the country.

KEY

⬭ **NOTABLE COFFEE-PRODUCING REGIONS**

▨ **AREA OF PRODUCTION**

0 km   150
0 miles   150

THAI COFFEE KEY FACTS

PERCENTAGE OF WORLD MARKET: **0.5%**

HARVEST: OCTOBER–MARCH

MAIN TYPES:
98% ROBUSTA
2% ARABICA
CATURRA, CATUAI, CATIMOR, GEISHA

PROCESSES: NATURAL, SOME WASHED

WORLD RANKING AS A PRODUCER: **21ST LARGEST PRODUCER IN THE WORLD**

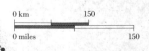

VIETNAM

There are some soft, sweet, and nutty varieties here that are of interest to the speciality market.

Vietnam began to produce coffee in 1857. In the early 1900s, after some political reforms, farmers boosted their coffee production to capitalize on good market prices. Over a 10-year period, Vietnam became the second-largest coffee producer in the world. As a result, inferior Robustas flooded the market, causing a low-price, low-quality trend. Today, the government aims for a balance between supply and demand. Robusta is the main crop, but a little Arabica also grows.

Washed Arabica
The flavour profile of Vietnamese Arabica is yet to be identified, as production is growing.

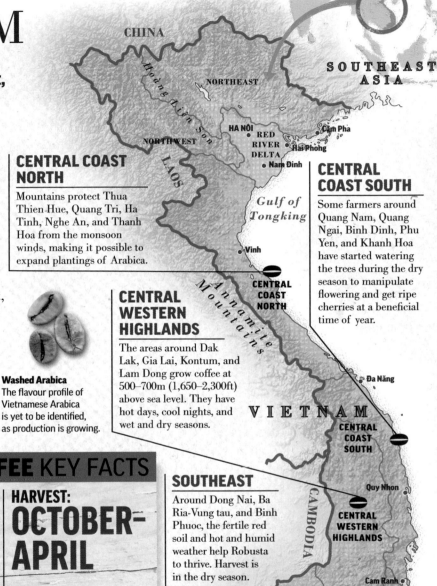

CENTRAL COAST NORTH

Mountains protect Thua Thien Hue, Quang Tri, Ha Tinh, Nghe An, and Thanh Hoa from the monsoon winds, making it possible to expand plantings of Arabica.

CENTRAL COAST SOUTH

Some farmers around Quang Nam, Quang Ngai, Binh Dinh, Phu Yen, and Khanh Hoa have started watering the trees during the dry season to manipulate flowering and get ripe cherries at a beneficial time of year.

CENTRAL WESTERN HIGHLANDS

The areas around Dak Lak, Gia Lai, Kontum, and Lam Dong grow coffee at 500–700m (1,650–2,300ft) above sea level. They have hot days, cool nights, and wet and dry seasons.

SOUTHEAST

Around Dong Nai, Ba Ria-Vung tau, and Binh Phuoc, the fertile red soil and hot and humid weather help Robusta to thrive. Harvest is in the dry season.

VIETNAMESE COFFEE KEY FACTS

PERCENTAGE OF WORLD MARKET: **14%**

MAIN TYPES: **95% ROBUSTA 5% ARABICA** CATIMOR, CHARI (EXCELSA)

HARVEST: **OCTOBER–APRIL**

PROCESSES: **NATURAL, SOME WASHED**

WORLD RANKING AS A PRODUCER: **2ND LARGEST PRODUCER IN THE WORLD**

KEY
- ⬭ NOTABLE COFFEE-PRODUCING REGIONS
- ▨ AREA OF PRODUCTION

0 km   150
0 miles   150

CHINA

Chinese coffees are generally soft and sweet, with delicate acidity and nutty flavours that can cross over into caramel and chocolate.

Coffee has been growing in China since 1887, when it was brought to Yunnan by missionaries. It took another century before the government focused efforts on its production. New measures have improved practices and conditions, helping total coffee production to grow by about 15 per cent every year. While the per capita is currently only 2–3 cups a year, this is also increasing. Arabica varieties grown here include Catimor and Typica.

YUNNAN PROVINCE

The Pu'er, Kunming, Lincang Wenshan, and Dehong regions grow 95 per cent of Chinese coffees. Most are Catimor, while some old Bourbon and Typica can still be found in the Baoshan prefecture. Coffees are mostly low-acidic, nutty, or cereal-like in taste.

ASIA

Washed Typica
China's Typica is often sweet, structured, and medium-bodied.

HAINAN ISLAND

Off the south coast of China, the island of Hainan grows about 300–400kg ($\frac{1}{3}$–$\frac{1}{2}$ tonne) of Robusta annually, and while production is in decline, coffee culture is very strong among the people here. The coffee is often mild, woody, and heavy-bodied.

Drying coffee cherries
It is not uncommon for families to dry cherries outside their homes, both to sell and consume.

Washed Catimor
This is the most widespread variety grown in China.

FUJIAN PROVINCE

The coastal province across from Taiwan is a large producer of tea, but some Robusta coffee is grown here, making up a small percentage of China's total output. Robustas are typically low in acidity and full-bodied.

KEY

⬤ **NOTABLE COFFEE-PRODUCING REGIONS**

▨ **AREA OF PRODUCTION**

0 km   400
0 miles   400

CHINESE COFFEE KEY FACTS

PERCENTAGE OF WORLD MARKET: **0.5%**

MAIN TYPES: **95% ARABICA** CATIMOR, BOURBON, TYPICA **5% ROBUSTA**

HARVEST: NOVEMBER–APRIL

PROCESSES: WASHED AND NATURAL

WORLD RANKING AS A PRODUCER: **20TH LARGEST PRODUCER**

YEMEN

Some of the most interesting Arabicas in the world grow in Yemen, with "wild" flavours of spice, earth, fruits, and tobacco.

Coffee grew in Yemen long before it reached any other country outside of Africa. The small town of Mocha was the first port to establish commerical export.

Coffee still grows wild in some places, but the main cultivated areas grow old Typica and old Ethiopian strains. Varieties often share the same name as regions, making it difficult to trace and identify them.

HARAZI

Half way to the coast from Sana'a, the Jabal Haraz mountain range is home to the Harazi coffee growers, who produce classically complex, fruity, wine-like coffee.

MATARI

Immediately to the west of Sana'a on the way to the port in Hodeidah, the area producing Matari coffee lies at a high altitude and is known to produce some of the more acidic Yemeni coffees.

ASIA

Empty Quarter

OMAN

SAUDI ARABIA

Ramlat Dahm

Red Sea

Al Mahrah

Y E M E N

MATARI
SANA'A

HARAZI

Hodeidah

ISMAILI

DHAMARI

Ramlat as Sab'atayn

Hadhramaut

Al Mukalla

Ta'izz

Gulf of Aden

Aden

Ripening coffee cherries
Yemeni coffees are often allowed to overripen and dry up on the branches.

YEMENI COFFEE KEY FACTS

PERCENTAGE OF WORLD MARKET: **0.1%**

MAIN TYPES:
ARABICA
TYPICA, HEIRLOOM

HARVEST:
JUNE–DECEMBER

PROCESS:
NATURAL

LOCAL TECHNIQUE

Growing and processing has remained unchanged for the past 800 years, and chemical use is uncommon. Due to the lack of water, coffees are naturally processed, and can look irregular.

WORLD RANKING AS A PRODUCER: **33RD LARGEST PRODUCER**

DHAMARI

South of Sana'a, the western districts of the Dhamar governorate produce coffees that have classic Yemeni traits, but are often softer and rounder than the western coffees.

ISMAILI

Named after a group of Muslims that settled in the area around Hutayb, Ismaili is both the name of a local variety and the general area, producing some of the more rustic Yemeni coffees.

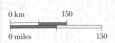

Natural Heirloom
Unknown Heirloom varieties are naturally processed here, adding a unique local character.

0 km   150

0 miles   150

KEY

 **NOTABLE COFFEE-PRODUCING REGIONS**

AREA OF PRODUCTION

COFFEES OF THE WORLD
SOUTH AND CENTRAL AMERICA

BRAZIL

Brazil is the world's largest producer of coffee. Regional differences are difficult to distinguish, but it is widely accepted that Brazil produces soft-washed Arabicas and sweet naturals with mild acidity and medium texture.

In 1920, Brazil produced about 80 per cent of all the coffee grown in the world. As other countries increased their production, Brazil's market share decreased to the current 35 per cent, but it remains the largest producer worldwide. It mainly grows Arabica – Mundo Novo and Icatu varieties, among others.

After the devastating frost of 1975, many farmers established new plantations in Minas Gerais, which now alone produces nearly half of Brazil's coffee – enough to rival the output of Vietnam, the second largest producer in the world. When Brazil has a peak or slump in production, it sends ripples through the market and affects the livelihoods of millions – the price we all pay for our cup of coffee.

Today, there are about 300,000 farms across the country, ranging in size from half a hectare to more than 10,000 hectares (25,000 acres). Brazil consumes about half of all the coffee it produces.

PRECISE PLANTINGS
Neat rows of trees on flat terrain help farmers to machine harvest – a key part of Brazil's farming system.

BRAZILIAN COFFEE KEY FACTS

PERCENTAGE OF WORLD MARKET: 35%

PROCESSES: NATURAL, PULPED NATURAL, SEMI WASHED, AND FULLY WASHED

MAIN TYPES: 80% ARABICA
BOURBON, CATUAI, ACAIA, MUNDO NOVO, ICATU
20% ROBUSTA

HARVEST: MAY–SEPTEMBER

WORLD RANKING AS A PRODUCER: LARGEST COFFEE PRODUCER IN THE WORLD

LOCAL TECHNIQUE
Much of the coffee-producing process in Brazil is heavily mechanized, and unlike many countries, they have a practice of harvesting first and sorting later.

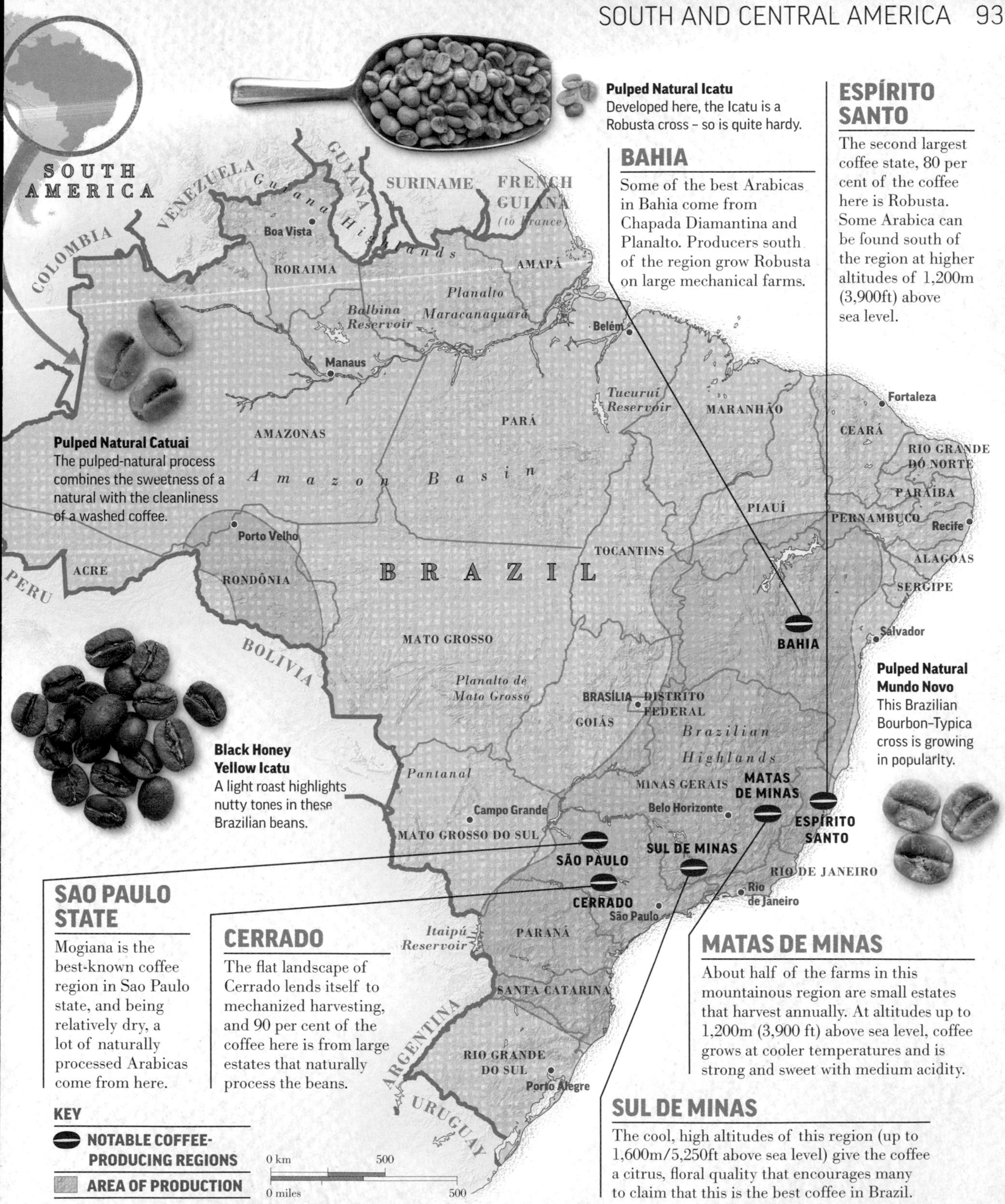

Pulped Natural Icatu
Developed here, the Icatu is a Robusta cross – so is quite hardy.

ESPÍRITO SANTO

The second largest coffee state, 80 per cent of the coffee here is Robusta. Some Arabica can be found south of the region at higher altitudes of 1,200m (3,900ft) above sea level.

BAHIA

Some of the best Arabicas in Bahia come from Chapada Diamantina and Planalto. Producers south of the region grow Robusta on large mechanical farms.

Pulped Natural Catuai
The pulped-natural process combines the sweetness of a natural with the cleanliness of a washed coffee.

Pulped Natural Mundo Novo
This Brazilian Bourbon–Typica cross is growing in popularity.

Black Honey Yellow Icatu
A light roast highlights nutty tones in these Brazilian beans.

SAO PAULO STATE

Mogiana is the best-known coffee region in Sao Paulo state, and being relatively dry, a lot of naturally processed Arabicas come from here.

CERRADO

The flat landscape of Cerrado lends itself to mechanized harvesting, and 90 per cent of the coffee here is from large estates that naturally process the beans.

MATAS DE MINAS

About half of the farms in this mountainous region are small estates that harvest annually. At altitudes up to 1,200m (3,900 ft) above sea level, coffee grows at cooler temperatures and is strong and sweet with medium acidity.

SUL DE MINAS

The cool, high altitudes of this region (up to 1,600m/5,250ft above sea level) give the coffee a citrus, floral quality that encourages many to claim that this is the best coffee in Brazil.

KEY

⬤ NOTABLE COFFEE-PRODUCING REGIONS

▨ AREA OF PRODUCTION

0 km   500

0 miles   500

Map labels: SOUTH AMERICA; COLOMBIA; VENEZUELA; Guyana Highlands; GUYANA; SURINAME; FRENCH GUIANA (to France); Boa Vista; RORAIMA; AMAPÁ; Planalto Maracanaquará; Balbina Reservoir; Manaus; Belém; MARANHÃO; Fortaleza; CEARÁ; AMAZONAS; PARÁ; Amazon Basin; Tucuruí Reservoir; RIO GRANDE DO NORTE; PARAÍBA; PERNAMBUCO; Recife; PIAUÍ; PERU; ACRE; Porto Velho; RONDÔNIA; BRAZIL; TOCANTINS; ALAGOAS; SERGIPE; BOLIVIA; MATO GROSSO; Planalto de Mato Grosso; BRASÍLIA; DISTRITO FEDERAL; GOIÁS; Brazilian Highlands; Salvador; BAHIA; Pantanal; Campo Grande; MATO GROSSO DO SUL; MINAS GERAIS; Belo Horizonte; MATAS DE MINAS; ESPÍRITO SANTO; SÃO PAULO; SUL DE MINAS; RIO DE JANEIRO; Rio de Janeiro; CERRADO; São Paulo; Itaipú Reservoir; PARANÁ; ARGENTINA; SANTA CATARINA; RIO GRANDE DO SUL; Porto Alegre; URUGUAY

COLOMBIA

Colombian coffees are generally rich and full bodied. They span a vast range of flavour attributes – from sweet, nutty, and chocolatey to floral, fruity, and almost tropical. Each region offers a distinct profile.

The mountains of Colombia create an abundance of microclimates that bring out potentially unique qualities in the coffee. All of the coffee is Arabica – including Typica and Bourbon varieties – and traditionally washed, and there are one or two harvests a year depending on the region. Some harvest the coffee cherries just from September to December, with another smaller harvest in April or May. Others harvest their main crop from March to June, and gain another crop from October to November. Two million Colombians rely on coffee for their livelihoods. Most of these people work for a group of small farms, but about 560,000 of them are producers who have only 1–2 hectares (2½–5 acres) of land. In recent years, the speciality industry has gained access to work with small farmers individually, buying small volumes and paying more for quality crops.

More and more Colombians drink Colombian coffee – around 20 per cent of the total coffee production.

DRYING BEANS
Beans usually dry on concrete, but where terrain is too steep, workers choose to dry them on rooftops.

COLOMBIAN COFFEE KEY FACTS

PERCENTAGE OF WORLD MARKET: **6%**

MAIN TYPES:

ARABICA

TYPICA, BOURBON, TABI, CATURRA, COLOMBIA, MARAGOGIPE, CASTILLO

CHALLENGES:
CONTROLLED DRYING, FINANCE, SOIL EROSION, CLIMATE CHANGE, LACK OF WATER, LACK OF SECURITY

HARVESTS:
MARCH–JUNE AND **SEPTEMBER–DECEMBER**

PROCESS:
WASHED

WORLD RANKING AS A PRODUCER: **4TH LARGEST COFFEE PRODUCER IN THE WORLD**

LOCAL TECHNIQUE
Most farmers have their own wet-milling facilities and so can control the drying process (see pp20–21). Raised beds are now popular – these help producers to turn beans easily as they dry.

SOUTH AMERICA

Washed Caturra
Light-to-medium roasts highlight the citrus notes of many Colombian coffees.

SANTANDER

One of the northernmost regions, Santander and Norte de Santander grow 9 per cent of the Colombian coffee, most of it under shade and at lower altitudes, resulting in softer, earthier coffees with low acidity.

Colombian coffee farm
Neatly planted in rows, Colombian coffee farms are often very well managed.

CAUCA

The best-known municipalities in Cauca are Inza and Popayan, and, as a whole, the department produces 8 per cent of Colombia's coffee, known to be sweet and light, with floral and berry notes.

Washed Tekisik
Originally from El Salvador, Tekisik is gaining popularity here.

NARIÑO

The southernmost of the coffee-growing departments, Nariño has gained a reputation for its smooth, creamy coffee, with stone-fruit overtones, though it grows only 3 per cent of Colombia's coffee.

TOLIMA

Known to supply soft, sweet coffees with occasional light and balanced floral notes, the Department of Tolima represents about 12 per cent of Colombian coffee production.

Washed Caturra and Bourbon
Both Bourbon and the more compact Caturra thrive in the Colombian climate, where most farmers grow a mix of varieties.

HUILA

12 per cent of the coffees from Colombia come from the mountains in Huila, a region that many hail as the best in the country. The coffees are often fruity, high in acidity, with a dense texture and a complex flavour.

KEY

● NOTABLE COFFEE-PRODUCING REGIONS

▦ AREA OF PRODUCTION

0 km 200
0 miles 200

BOLIVIA

There are few known regional flavour profiles in Bolivia, but coffees can be sweet and balanced, floral and herbal, or creamy and chocolatey. It is a small coffee producer with the potential to grow stunning varieties.

With a coffee culture that includes around 23,000 small, family-run farms of 2–9 hectares (5–20 acres) each, Bolivia consumes around 40 per cent of the coffee it produces.

Bolivian coffees have only recently captured the interest of speciality buyers, as internal challenges of transport, processing, and lack of technical support make quality unpredictable. Most coffee for export is shipped out via Peru, as Bolivia is landlocked, adding to its logistical challenges. Investment in education and new processing facilities near growing regions have improved quality, and exporters are starting to explore international markets.

Bolivia mainly grows Arabica varieties, such as Typica, Caturra, and Catuai. Coffee grows organically almost everywhere. Main regions of production are La Paz provinces, such as North and South Yungas, Franz Tamayo, Caranavi, Inquisivi, and Larecaja. Harvest times vary, as they depend on altitudes, rainfall patterns, and temperatures.

GROWING AND HARVEST
A lot of Bolivian coffee is organic by default, as growers have little or no funds for chemicals.

BOLIVIAN COFFEE KEY FACTS

PERCENTAGE OF WORLD MARKET: LESS THAN **0.1%**

MAIN TYPES:
ARABICA
TYPICA, CATURRA, CRIOLLO, CATUAI, CATIMOR

PROCESSES:
WASHED, SOME NATURAL

HARVEST:
JULY–NOVEMBER

CHALLENGES:
UNRELIABLE TRANSPORT, LACK OF PROCESSING EQUIPMENT AND TECHNICAL SUPPORT

WORLD RANKING AS A PRODUCER: **35TH LARGEST COFFEE PRODUCER IN THE WORLD**

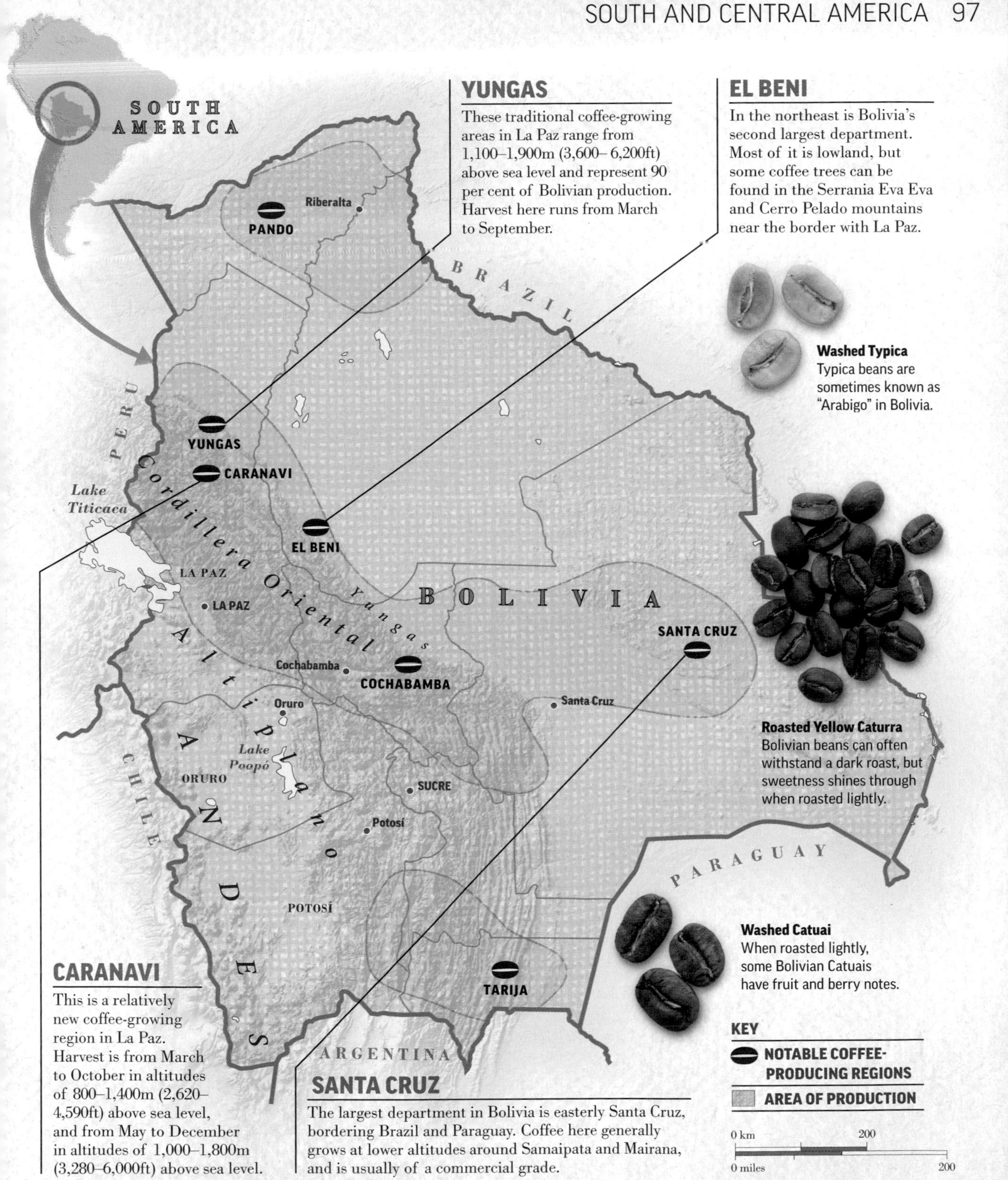
SOUTH AMERICA
PANDO
Riberalta
BRAZIL
PERU
YUNGAS
CARANAVI
Lake Titicaca
Cordillera Oriental
EL BENI
LA PAZ
LA PAZ
Yungas
BOLIVIA
SANTA CRUZ
Altiplano
Cochabamba
COCHABAMBA
Santa Cruz
Oruro
Lake Poopó
ORURO
CHILE
ANDES
SUCRE
Potosí
POTOSÍ
PARAGUAY
TARIJA
ARGENTINA
KEY
NOTABLE COFFEE-PRODUCING REGIONS
AREA OF PRODUCTION
0 km
200
0 miles
200

YUNGAS

These traditional coffee-growing areas in La Paz range from 1,100–1,900m (3,600– 6,200ft) above sea level and represent 90 per cent of Bolivian production. Harvest here runs from March to September.

EL BENI

In the northeast is Bolivia's second largest department. Most of it is lowland, but some coffee trees can be found in the Serrania Eva Eva and Cerro Pelado mountains near the border with La Paz.

Washed Typica
Typica beans are sometimes known as "Arabigo" in Bolivia.

Roasted Yellow Caturra
Bolivian beans can often withstand a dark roast, but sweetness shines through when roasted lightly.

Washed Catuai
When roasted lightly, some Bolivian Catuais have fruit and berry notes.

CARANAVI

This is a relatively new coffee-growing region in La Paz. Harvest is from March to October in altitudes of 800–1,400m (2,620–4,590ft) above sea level, and from May to December in altitudes of 1,000–1,800m (3,280–6,000ft) above sea level.

SANTA CRUZ

The largest department in Bolivia is easterly Santa Cruz, bordering Brazil and Paraguay. Coffee here generally grows at lower altitudes around Samaipata and Mairana, and is usually of a commercial grade.

PERU

A small number of well-textured, balanced coffees with earthy, herbal notes are produced in Peru.

Despite its high-quality coffees, Peru faces problems of inconsistent standards. A major cause is the lack of internal logistics, but the government continues to invest in education and infrastructure, such as roads, as well as in new growing areas – especially in the north, where new Arabica is grown.

Peru mainly grows varieties of Arabica, such as Typica, Bourbon, and Caturra. Around 90 per cent of the coffee is grown on around 120,000 small farms, most of them cultivating approximately 2 hectares (5 acres) each.

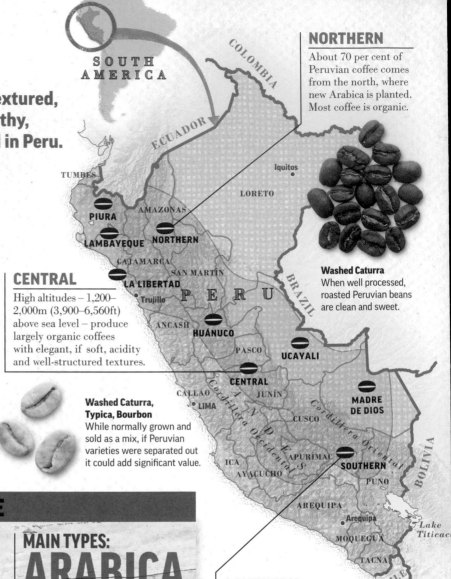

SOUTH AMERICA

NORTHERN
About 70 per cent of Peruvian coffee comes from the north, where new Arabica is planted. Most coffee is organic.

Washed Caturra
When well processed, roasted Peruvian beans are clean and sweet.

CENTRAL
High altitudes – 1,200–2,000m (3,900–6,560ft) above sea level – produce largely organic coffees with elegant, if soft, acidity and well-structured textures.

Washed Caturra, Typica, Bourbon
While normally grown and sold as a mix, if Peruvian varieties were separated out it could add significant value.

SOUTHERN
This is the smallest coffee-growing region in Peru. Most of the coffees are sold in bulk or through cooperatives, making it difficult to trace them.

KEY
⬤ **NOTABLE COFFEE-PRODUCING REGIONS**
▨ **AREA OF PRODUCTION**

0 km — 300
0 miles — 300

PERUVIAN COFFEE

PERCENTAGE OF WORLD MARKET: **3%**

HARVEST: MAY–SEPTEMBER

PROCESS: WASHED

MAIN TYPES:
ARABICA
TYPICA, BOURBON, CATURRA, PACHE, CATIMOR

WORLD RANKING AS A PRODUCER:
9TH LARGEST COFFEE PRODUCER IN THE WORLD

ECUADOR

SOUTH AMERICA

Varied ecosystems result in coffees that range in flavour, but most display classic South American qualities.

These qualities include a medium body, structured acidity, and pleasant sweetness. The Ecuador coffee industry faces challenges – the lack of credit facilities, low yields, and high labour costs are detrimental to quality. The overall area under cultivation has halved since 1985. It produces Robusta and low-quality Arabica. Most coffee is shade-grown and organic, and most smallholdings have their own wet mills. Still, the potential for quality is present in the highest altitudes, and in addition to Typica and Bourbon varieties, plantings of Caturra, Catuai, Pacas, and Sarchimor are taking place.

Washed Robusta
While naturally processed beans still dominate, washed Robustas are on the increase.

MANABÍ

This is the largest coffee-growing area, producing 50 per cent of Ecuador's Arabica, both washed and natural. Coffee in this dry, coastal area grows at modest altitudes of 300–700m (1,000–2,300ft) above sea level.

ESMERALDAS
Esmeraldas
CARCHI
COLOMBIA
IMBABURA
QUITO
PICHINCHA
SUCUMBÍOS
NAPO
COTOPAXI
E C U A D O R
ORELLANA
MANABÍ
Portoviejo
TUNGURAHUA
LOS RÍOS
BOLÍVAR
Riobamba
PASTAZA
CHIMBORAZO
GUAYAS
Guayaquil
CAÑAR
MORONA SANTIAGO
AZUAY
EL ORO
PERU
LOJA
ZAMORA CHINCHIPE
Loja

Washed Typica
Most coffee trees are replaced after 10–15 years, but many trees in Ecuador are more than 40 years old.

ZAMORA CHINCHIPE

This southeastern region benefits from altitudes of 1,000–1,800m (3,280–6,000ft) above sea level, and produces mainly washed Arabicas that can be bright and sweet with hints of berries.

ECUADORIAN COFFEE

PERCENTAGE OF WORLD MARKET: 0.5%

MAIN TYPES:
60% ARABICA
40% ROBUSTA

PROCESSES: WASHED AND NATURAL

HARVEST: MAY–SEPTEMBER

WORLD RANKING AS A PRODUCER: 19TH

LOJA AND EL ORO

Old growing regions in the south, ranging from 500–1,800m (1,640–6,000ft) above sea level, produce 20 per cent of Ecuador's Arabica. Being a dry area, 90 per cent of it is naturally processed.

KEY

⬤ NOTABLE COFFEE-PRODUCING REGIONS

▒ AREA OF PRODUCTION

0 km   100
0 miles   100

DECAFFEINATED COFFEE

Many myths surround caffeinated and decaffeinated coffee, their health benefits, and health risks. For those who love and appreciate the flavour of good coffee, but would like to reduce their caffeine intake, there are options.

IS CAFFEINE BAD FOR YOU?

Caffeine, a purine alkaloid, is an odourless, slightly bitter compound, which in pure form is an extremely toxic white powder. In natural, brewed-coffee form, caffeine is a common stimulant that, once ingested, rapidly affects the central nervous system and equally rapidly leaves the body. Its effects vary from person to person. It can increase your metabolism and give you a feeling of reduced fatigue, but it can also increase nervousness. Depending on your gender, weight, genetic heritage, and medical history, caffeine can be a positive pick-me-up or cause levels of discomfort, so it is important to have an awareness of how it makes you feel and the affect on your health.

HOW DO THE BEANS COMPARE?

Green decaf beans are darker green or brown in colour. The darker hue is also apparent, but less noticeable, when they have been roasted. Due to weakened cell structure, you may see a sheen of oil on the surface of a light-roasted decaf. It may also appear smoother or more even in colour.

COFFEE BEANS

Unroasted
Guatemala
Bourbon

Roasted
Guatemala
Bourbon

DECAFFEINATED COFFEE BEANS

Unroasted
Mountain
Water decaf,
Guatemala
Bourbon

Roasted
Mountain Water
decaf, Guatemala
Bourbon

THE TRUTH ABOUT DECAF

Decaffeinated coffee is readily available in most shops and cafes, and generally has 90–99 per cent of the caffeine removed, reducing the level down to well below that of a cup of black tea, and to about the same as a mug of hot chocolate.

Sadly, most decaffeinated coffee is made from old or poor-quality green beans, and often comes darkly roasted to cover up the unpleasant flavours. If you find a supplier that decaffeinates fresh, good-quality green coffee beans and roasts them well, the flavour will not be compromised. You may not be able to tell the difference between a regular and a decaf and can enjoy it without any ill effect.

THE SCIENCE BIT

There are different methods of decaffeination – some introduce solvents and others rely on more natural processes. Look out for this information on decaf coffee bean labels.

SOLVENTS PROCESS

The beans are steamed or soaked in hot water to open up the cell structure. Ethyl acetate and methylene chloride are then used to rinse the caffeine out of the beans or from the water in which they were soaked. These solvents are not highly selective and can sometimes remove positive attributes from the coffee, and the process can damage the structure of the bean causing challenges in storing and roasting.

SWISS WATER PROCESS

The beans are soaked in water to open up the cell structure. A water-based green coffee extract, or water saturated with green coffee compounds, is used to wash the caffeine out. The extract is then filtered through carbon to remove the caffeine and re-used to extract more caffeine until the desired level is reached. Chemical-free, this process is gentle on the bean and leaves much of its natural flavour intact.

The Mountain Water method is nearly identical in process, but is produced in Mexico using water from the Pico de Orizaba mountain.

CO$_2$ PROCESS

Liquid CO_2 is used at low temperature and pressure to extract the caffeine from the cells of the bean. This disrupts very little of the compounds that affect the flavour of the coffee. The caffeine is filtered or evaporated from the CO_2, and the liquid is re-used to further extract more caffeine out of the beans. Preserving the natural flavours of the beans, this process is chemical-free, gentle, and considered organic.

CO$_2$ PROCESS DECAF BEANS
This process leaves beans smooth and glossy with a deep green colour.

GUATEMALA

Guatemalan coffees offer some exceptionally varied regional flavour profiles – ranging from sweet with cocoa and toffee notes, to herbal, citrus, or floral coffees that display a crisp acidity.

There are many microclimates here – from the mountain ranges to the plains – and these, with the varied rainfall patterns and rich soils, create coffee with a huge range of flavours.

Coffee grows in nearly all of the departments, and the Guatemalan National Coffee Association has identified eight main regions that offer distinct profiles. Within these regions there are great variations in aroma and flavour, influenced by varieties and local microclimates. Around 270,000 hectares (670,000

acres) is dedicated to growing coffee varieties, almost all of which are washed Arabica, such as Bourbon and Caturra. A small amount of Robusta grows at lower altitudes in the southwest. There are nearly 100,000 producers, most of whom have small farms of 2–3 hectares (5–7 acres) each. Most farms deliver their coffee cherries to a wet mill for processing (see pp20–23), but it is increasingly common for producers to have their own small beneficios (processing plants).

HILLSIDE PLANTATION
The lush hillsides of high-altitude Guatemalan coffee regions are often laced with clouds.

GUATEMALAN COFFEE KEY FACTS

PERCENTAGE OF WORLD MARKET: AROUND **2.5%**

MAIN TYPES:
98% ARABICA
BOURBON, CATURRA, CATUAI, TYPICA, MARAGOGIPE, PACHE
2% ROBUSTA

PROCESSES:
WASHED, SMALL AMOUNTS OF **NATURAL**

HARVEST:
NOVEMBER–APRIL

WORLD RANKING AS A PRODUCER: **10TH LARGEST COFFEE PRODUCER IN THE WORLD**

LOCAL TECHNIQUE
"Injerto reina" is a technique that grafts the stem of an Arabica tree onto the root of a Robusta tree. This helps the Arabica tree to become disease-resistant without losing its flavour.

CENTRAL AMERICA

Lacandón Mountains

PETÉN

Flores

Washed Bourbon
The Bourbon variety is thought to have been the first coffee variety produced in Guatemala.

HUEHUETENANGO

The non-volcanic highlands of Huehue are at the highest altitude in Guatemala, with little rainfall and a late harvest season. The coffee has a floral and fruity flavour and is often considered the best and most complex that Guatemala can offer.

Washed Red Catuai
Catuai trees are popular in Guatemala; they are compact, resilient, and high yielding.

Maya Mountains

BELIZE

COBÁN

Covered by rainforest, the altitude in Cobán is 1,300–1,400m (4,260–4,590ft) above sea level, but temperatures are low and rainfall and humidity high. The resulting coffee is heavy and balanced, fruity, and sometimes spicy.

MEXICO

Gulf of Honduras

G U A T E M A L A

HUEHUETENANGO

QUICHÉ   ALTA VERAPAZ

COBÁN

IZABAL   Puerto Barrios

Lake Izabal

Chuacús Mountains   BAJA VERAPAZ   *Las Minas Mountains*

TOTONICAPÁN *Sierra*   ZACAPA

SAN MARCOS

QUEZALTENANGO   EL PROGRESO   *Madre*

Quezaltenango   GUATEMALA

SOLOLÁ CHIMALTENANGO   CHIQUIMULA

ATITLÁN Lake Atitlán   ACATENANGO

                    GUATEMALA CITY

SACATEPÉQUEZ   JALAPA

RETALHULEU   ANTIGUA   FRAIJUNES

                    NUEVO ORIENTE

Escuintla   JUTIAPA

SUCHITEPÉQUEZ

ESCUINTLA   SANTA ROSA

Washed Caturra
Local farms here take care to separate varieties to highlight individual flavour characteristics.

KEY

⬛ **NOTABLE COFFEE-PRODUCING REGIONS**

▨ **AREA OF PRODUCTION**

0 km   50
0 miles   50

ATITLÁN

On a level with Antigua, but with a little more rain and higher humidity, the areas around Lake Atitlán produce coffee that is often thought of as classic Guatemalan: bright and citric, chocolatey, full bodied, and fragrant.

ANTIGUA

The first coffee-producing region in Guatemala, these valley coffees grow at 1,300–1,600m (4,260–5,250ft) above sea level. The weather is cool and dry, and the coffee is sweet and balanced with nutty, spicy, and chocolatey notes.

ACATENANGO

At one of the highest altitudes of 1,300–2,000m (4,260–6,560ft) above sea level, Acatenango is hot and dry with rich volcanic soils. The coffee tends to be high in acidity and very complex.

EL SALVADOR

Producing some of the most flavoursome coffees in the world, El Salvador's coffee is sweet and creamy, with dried fruit, citrus, chocolate, and caramel notes.

The very first Arabica varieties to arrive in El Salvador were left undisturbed on farms while the country went through political and economical challenges. Almost two-thirds of the coffee grown now is Bourbon, the remaining one-third being mostly Pacas, and some Pacamara – a popular cross created in El Salvador.

There are about 20,000 growers in El Salvador – 95 per cent of whom have small farms of less than 20 hectares (50 acres) that are about 500–1,200m (1,640–3,900ft) above sea level. Nearly half of these farms can be found in the Apaneca-Llamatepec region. As coffee is grown in the shade, coffee plantations have played a vital part in the battle against deforestation and loss of habitats for wildlife. If you removed these trees, El Salvador would have virtually no natural forest left.

In recent years, the growers have focused largely on improving the quality of their coffee and marketing it to speciality buyers – creating a trade that better withstands the fluctuations of the commodity market.

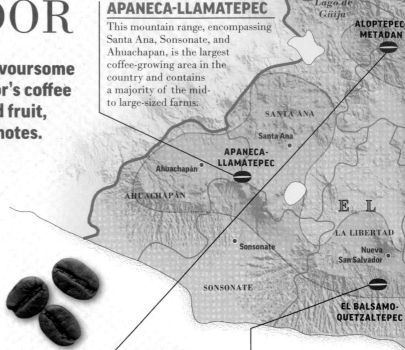

APANECA-LLAMATEPEC

This mountain range, encompassing Santa Ana, Sonsonate, and Ahuachapan, is the largest coffee-growing area in the country and contains a majority of the mid- to large-sized farms.

Washed Bourbon (CO$_2$ Decaf)
Fresh, highland grown, intensely flavoured beans are best suited to withstand the decaffeination process.

ALOPTEPEC-METAPAN

This small volcanic region in the northwest includes well-known departments such as Santa Ana and Chalatenango. It has the fewest farms, but is often considered to produce some of the best coffees.

EL BALSAMO-QUETZALTEPEC

In the southern parts of the central belt, the Balsamo Range and San Salvador volcano are home to nearly 4,000 growers who produce full-bodied coffees with a classic Central American balance.

KEY

⬛ **NOTABLE COFFEE-PRODUCING REGIONS**

▨ **AREA OF PRODUCTION**

0 km — 30
0 miles — 30

COFFEE PLANTATION
Coffee is often intercropped with false banana, other fruit trees, or trees grown for timber production.

Washed Pacamara
A cross of Pacas and Maragogype, the Pacamara is often herbal and savoury in taste.

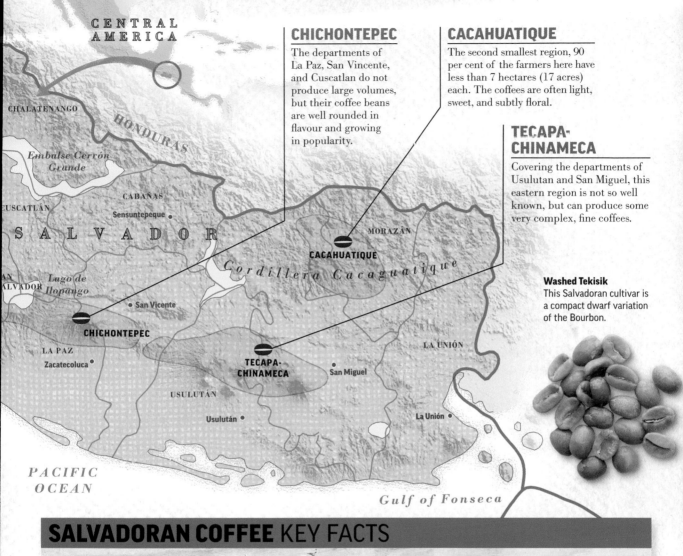

CHICHONTEPEC

The departments of La Paz, San Vincente, and Cuscatlan do not produce large volumes, but their coffee beans are well rounded in flavour and growing in popularity.

CACAHUATIQUE

The second smallest region, 90 per cent of the farmers here have less than 7 hectares (17 acres) each. The coffees are often light, sweet, and subtly floral.

TECAPA-CHINAMECA

Covering the departments of Usulutan and San Miguel, this eastern region is not so well known, but can produce some very complex, fine coffees.

Washed Tekisik
This Salvadoran cultivar is a compact dwarf variation of the Bourbon.

SALVADORAN COFFEE KEY FACTS

PERCENTAGE OF WORLD MARKET: 0.9%

HARVEST: OCTOBER–MARCH

PROCESSES: WASHED, SOME NATURAL

MAIN TYPES: ARABICA
BOURBON, PACAS, PACAMARA, CATURRA, CATUAI, CATISIC

WORLD RANKING AS A PRODUCER: 15TH LARGEST COFFEE PRODUCER IN THE WORLD

COSTA RICA

CENTRAL AMERICA

Costa Rican coffees are delicious and easy to drink. They display a complex sweetness combined with refined acidity, mellow textures, and a range of citrus, floral flavours.

Taking great pride in the coffee it grows and produces, Costa Rica has banned Robusta production to protect its Arabica varieties, such as Typica, Caturra, and Villa Sarchi. The government has also issued strict environmental guidelines to protect vulnerable ecosystems and the future of coffee production.

There are more than 50,000 coffee growers in Costa Rica, and around 90 per cent of them are small producers with less than 5 hectares (12 acres) each. The industry has gone through something of a revolution in the production of quality coffee. Numerous micro-mills have been built around growing regions, allowing single producers or small groups of farmers to process their own beans, control and add value to their crop, and trade directly with buyers around the world.

This development has helped younger generations to continue family farms in spite of unstable markets – a trend that is sadly not common everywhere in the world.

Lake Nicaragu

Península Santa Elena

Cordillera de Guanacaste

Gulf of Papagayo

Liberia

GUANACASTE

Península de Nicoya

Yellow Honey Villalobos
The natural sweetness of the Villalobos can be intensified further by the honey process.

COSTA RICAN COFFEE KEY FACTS

PERCENTAGE OF WORLD MARKET: **1%**

HARVEST: VARIES FROM REGION TO REGION

PROCESSESES: WASHED, HONEY, NATURAL

WORLD RANKING AS A PRODUCER: **14TH LARGEST COFFEE PRODUCER IN THE WORLD**

MAIN TYPES:
ARABICA
TYPICA, CATURRA, CATUAI, VILLA SARCHI, BOURBON, GESHA, VILLALOBOS

LOCAL TECHNIQUE
The term "honey process" is used in Costa Rica to describe the pulped natural process (see p20), when varying degrees of pulp are left on the parchment. Honeys are white, yellow, red, black, or gold.

Yellow Honey Villa Sarchi
The fruity and floral tones of the Villa Sarchi make it one of the most unique Costa Rican varieties.

CENTRAL VALLEY

This was the first region to grow coffee in Central America, and is now also the most populated. Most coffee grows at 1,000–1,400m (3,280–4,590ft) above sea level, and harvest takes place from November to March.

Washed Catuai
Most Costa Rican coffees are washed, tasting bright and crisp even after roasting.

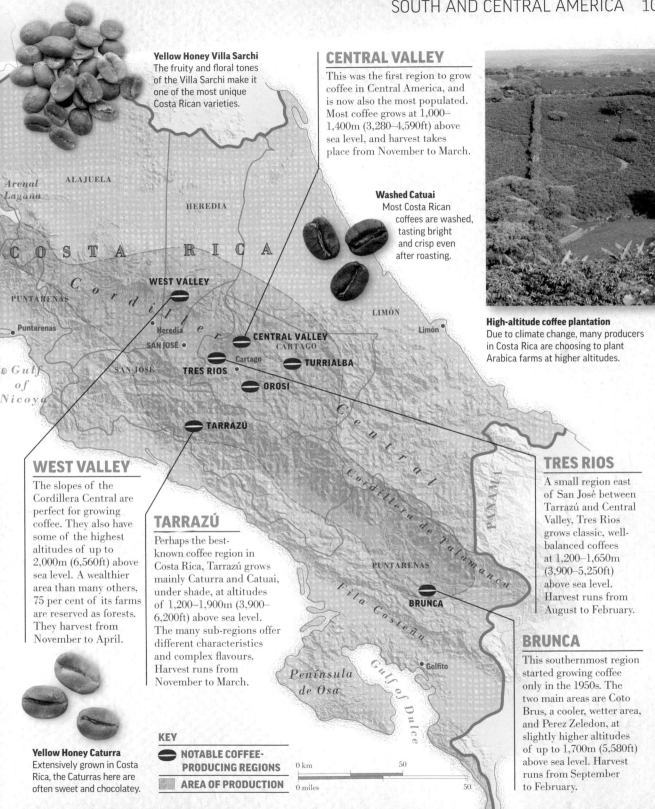

High-altitude coffee plantation
Due to climate change, many producers in Costa Rica are choosing to plant Arabica farms at higher altitudes.

WEST VALLEY

The slopes of the Cordillera Central are perfect for growing coffee. They also have some of the highest altitudes of up to 2,000m (6,560ft) above sea level. A wealthier area than many others, 75 per cent of its farms are reserved as forests. They harvest from November to April.

TARRAZÚ

Perhaps the best-known coffee region in Costa Rica, Tarrazú grows mainly Caturra and Catuai, under shade, at altitudes of 1,200–1,900m (3,900–6,200ft) above sea level. The many sub-regions offer different characteristics and complex flavours. Harvest runs from November to March.

Yellow Honey Caturra
Extensively grown in Costa Rica, the Caturras here are often sweet and chocolatey.

TRES RIOS

A small region east of San José between Tarrazú and Central Valley, Tres Rios grows classic, well-balanced coffees at 1,200–1,650m (3,900–5,250ft) above sea level. Harvest runs from August to February.

BRUNCA

This southernmost region started growing coffee only in the 1950s. The two main areas are Coto Brus, a cooler, wetter area, and Perez Zeledon, at slightly higher altitudes of up to 1,700m (5,580ft) above sea level. Harvest runs from September to February.

KEY

NOTABLE COFFEE-PRODUCING REGIONS

AREA OF PRODUCTION

0 km   50
0 miles   50

NICARAGUA

The best Nicaraguan coffees show a range of flavours – from sweet, fudge, and milk chocolate to more floral, delicate and acidic, herbal, savoury, and honeyed – and specific flavour profiles vary from region to region.

There is no doubt that this large, thinly populated country is capable of growing excellent coffees. However, between devastating hurricanes and political and financial instability, both the production of coffee and its reputation have suffered. Nevertheless, as coffee is the main export, producers are keen to resurrect its standing in speciality markets and continue to work on enhancing their agricultural practices within an improving infrastructure.

There are about 40,000 growers in Nicaragua, 80 per cent of whom have farms of fewer than 3 hectares (7 acres) each, at altitudes of 800–1,900m (2,620–6,200ft) above sea level. Most coffee grown here is Arabica, including varieties such as Bourbon and Pacamara. They are usually organic due to lack of funds for chemicals. The growers are hard to trace because they sell their coffee to large mills for processing, but single farms are beginning to trade directly with specialist buyers.

INCREASING YIELD
Farmers are starting to prune and fertilize more effectively to increase the yield of their coffee trees.

NICARAGUAN COFFEE KEY FACTS

PERCENTAGE OF WORLD MARKET: **1.2%**

HARVEST: **OCTOBER-MARCH**

MAIN TYPES: **ARABICA**
CATURRA, BOURBON, PACAMARA, MARAGOGYPE, MARACATURRA, CATUAI, CATIMOR

PROCESSES: **WASHED, SOME NATURAL, AND PULPED NATURAL**

WORLD RANKING AS A PRODUCER: **13TH LARGEST COFFEE PRODUCER IN THE WORLD**

NUEVA SEGOVIA

This region consistently produces some of the finest coffees: high in acidity, well structured, with a balanced sweetness and a complex range of spices and dried fruits.

JINOTEGA

Though it is the second largest department, Jinotega produces the most coffee. Often high in acidity, but with a light texture, it displays cocoa and berry notes.

Washed Red Catuai
As in other countries, Nicaraguan Catuai trees can grow either red or yellow fruit.

CENTRAL AMERICA

Washed Caturra
Caturra grows in large areas – sweet and nutty tasting.

HONDURAS

REGIÓN AUTÓNOMA ATLÁNTICO NORTE

Puerto Cabezas

Caribbean Sea

NUEVA SEGOVIA
● Ocotal

JINOTEGA

MADRIZ

ESTELÍ

Lake Apanás

Jinotega

MATAGALPA

Cordillera Isabella

Washed Pacamara
Roasted Pacamaras from Nicaragua are often herbal and high in acidity.

CHINANDEGA

● Chinandega

LEÓN

N I C A R A G U A

León ●

Lake Managua

BOACO

REGIÓN AUTÓNOMA ATLÁNTICO SUR

PACIFIC OCEAN

MANAGUA

MANAGUA

MASAYA

CHONTALES

● Juigalpa

Bluefields

Masaya ●

● Granada

MADRIZ

A small and relatively unknown area that was formerly part of Nueva Segovia, Madriz grows a modest amount of light, elegant coffees with great potential.

CARAZO

GRANADA

Lake Nicaragua

Ometepe Island

RÍO SAN JUAN

RIVAS

ESTELÍ

This small region might not be well known, but it produces great coffee – balanced and sweet with a velvety texture, floral aromas, and yellow fruit notes.

MATAGALPA

With a controlled citric acidity, creamy texture, delicate floral notes, and pronounced sweetness, Matagalpa produces some of the best coffees in Nicaragua.

KEY

● **NOTABLE COFFEE-PRODUCING REGIONS**

▨ **AREA OF PRODUCTION**

0 km   50

0 miles   50

Washed Maracaturra
A cross of Maragogype and Caturra. These big beans can sometimes taste like Kenyan coffee, even when grown here.

Mosquito Coast

HONDURAS

Some of the most contrasting flavour profiles in Central America are produced in Honduras – from soft, low-acid, nutty, and toffee-like, to highly acidic Kenyan-style coffees.

Honduras is capable of growing very clean, complex coffees, but suffers from poor infrastructure and a lack of controlled drying facilities.

Over half of the coffee comes from just three departments. Smallholdings mainly grow varieties of Arabica, including Pacas and Typica. Coffee is often organic by default, and nearly all of it is shade grown. To promote local speciality coffee, the National Coffee Institute is investing in training and education.

PLANTATION IN AGALTA
Coffee trees were first planted in Olancho, and now grow in nearly every department of Honduras.

Washed Pacas
Honduran Pacas are often well balanced with complex, fruity aromas.

KEY

⬛ **NOTABLE COFFEE-PRODUCING REGIONS**

▨ **AREA OF PRODUCTION**

0 km   50
0 miles   50

MONTECILLOS

This area covers the department of La Paz, parts of Comayagua, Intibucá, and Santa Barbara. It boasts some of the highest-altitude farms in Honduras resulting in bright, citrus, and well-structured coffees.

COPÁN

The departments of Copán, Ocotepeque, Cortés, Santa Barbara, and part of Lempira, make up the Copán profile of full-bodied coffees with cocoa and heavy sweetness.

AGALTA

Agalta spans the departments of Olancho and Yoro. Coffees here are sometimes tropical and sweet, with high acidity and chocolatey notes.

HONDURAN COFFEE

PERCENTAGE OF WORLD MARKET:	**3%**	**PROCESS:** WASHED
		MAIN TYPES: ARABICA
HARVEST: NOVEMBER–APRIL		CATURRA, CATUAI, PACAS, TYPICA

WORLD RANKING AS A PRODUCER: 7TH LARGEST PRODUCER IN THE WORLD

PANAMA

Panamanian coffees are sweet and balanced, at times floral or citrus, well-rounded, and easy to drink. Unusual varieties, such as Geisha, are very expensive.

Washed Caturra
This variety is found throughout the country, but is prevalent in Chiriqui.

Most coffee grows in the western province of Chiriqui, where climate and fertile soils are perfect conditions, and the high altitudes of the Baru volcano aid slow ripening. This area mainly grows Arabica varieties, such as Caturra and Typica. Farms are small- to medium-sized and family-run, and the country has good processing facilities and a well-developed infrastructure.

Development threatens farmland, so the future looks treacherous for coffee here.

CENTRAL AMERICA

VOLCAN
Some of the highest located farms are found here. Regular rainfall and rich soils mean the Baru coffees are often particularly complex and sweet.

"Wine" process mixed varieties
The local "wine" process allows cherries to overripen on the trees.

COSTA RICA

BOCAS DEL TORO

RENACIMIENTO

VOLCAN   BOQUETE

CHIRIQUÍ   David

Gulf of Chiriqui

NGÖBE BUGLE

Cordillera Central

PANAMA

VERAGUAS
Santiago

Chitré

HERRERA

Azuero Peninsula

LOS SANTOS

COCLÉ

COLÓN

Colón

Lake Gatún

PANAMÁ

Lake Bayano

PANAMA CITY   San Miguelito

KUNA DE WARGANDÍ

KUNA DE MADUNGANDÍ

Gulf of Darien

SAN BLAS

Bay of Panama

Pearl Islands

La Palma

EMBERÁ WOUNAAN

DARIÉN

EMBERÁ-WOUNAAN

Coiba

Washed Geisha
Due to its success in Panama, Geishas are now planted around the world.

RENACIMIENTO
Panama's most northern coffee-growing region, Renacimiento is hard to reach and less well known. Right on the border with Costa Rica, Renacimiento has farms up to 2,000m (6,560ft) above sea level with great potential for clean, high-acidity coffees.

BOQUETE
The oldest and best-known district for coffee in Panama – cool and misty and home to some of the most highly priced coffees in the world. Flavours range from cocoa to fruity with subtle acidity.

KEY
⬛ **NOTABLE COFFEE-PRODUCING REGIONS**
⬛ **AREA OF PRODUCTION**

0 km   50
0 miles   50

PANAMANIAN COFFEE

PERCENTAGE OF WORLD MARKET: **0.08%**

PROCESSES: **WASHED AND NATURAL**

WORLD RANKING AS A PRODUCER: **36TH**

MAIN TYPES:
ARABICA
CATURRA, CATUAI, TYPICA, GEISHA, MUNDO NOVO
SOME ROBUSTA

HARVEST: **DECEMBER–MARCH**

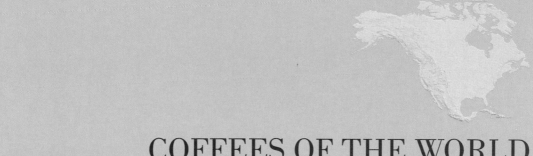

COFFEES OF THE WORLD
CARIBBEAN AND NORTH AMERICA

MEXICO

Coffees from Mexico are slowly emerging on the speciality market, gaining popularity for their sweet, soft, mild, and balanced flavours.

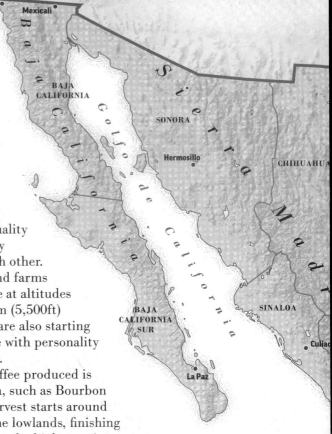

About 70 per cent of Mexican coffee is grown 400–900m (1,300–2,950ft) above sea level. The coffee industry involves more than 300,000 people, most of whom are producers with small farms that are less than 25 hectares (60 acres) in size. Low yields, limited financial support, poor infrastructure, and little technical assistance make it difficult for producers to improve quality. However, speciality coffee buyers and producers with the potential to grow high-quality coffee are slowly discovering each other. Cooperatives and farms that grow coffee at altitudes reaching 1,700m (5,500ft) above sea level are also starting to export coffee with personality and complexity.

Almost all coffee produced is washed Arabica, such as Bourbon and Typica. Harvest starts around November in the lowlands, finishing around March in the higher regions.

MEXICAN COFFEE KEY FACTS

PERCENTAGE OF WORLD MARKET: 3%

MAIN TYPES:
90% ARABICA
BOURBON, TYPICA, CATURRA, MUNDO NOVO, MARAGOGYPE, CATIMOR, CATUAI, GARNICA
10% ROBUSTA

HARVEST:
NOVEMBER–MARCH

PROCESSES:
WASHED, SOME NATURAL

CHALLENGES:
LOW YIELDS, LIMITED FINANCIAL AND **TECHNICAL SUPPORT, POOR INFRASTRUCTURE**

WORLD RANKING AS A PRODUCER: 8TH LARGEST COFFEE PRODUCER IN THE WORLD

NORTH
AMERICA

Washed Caturra, Catuai, Bourbon
Mexican farmers often grow
several varieties side by side.

Coffee seedlings in a nursery
In Mexico, as in most other countries and regions,
coffee-tree seedlings start life growing in a nursery
(see pp16–17), protected under shade cover.

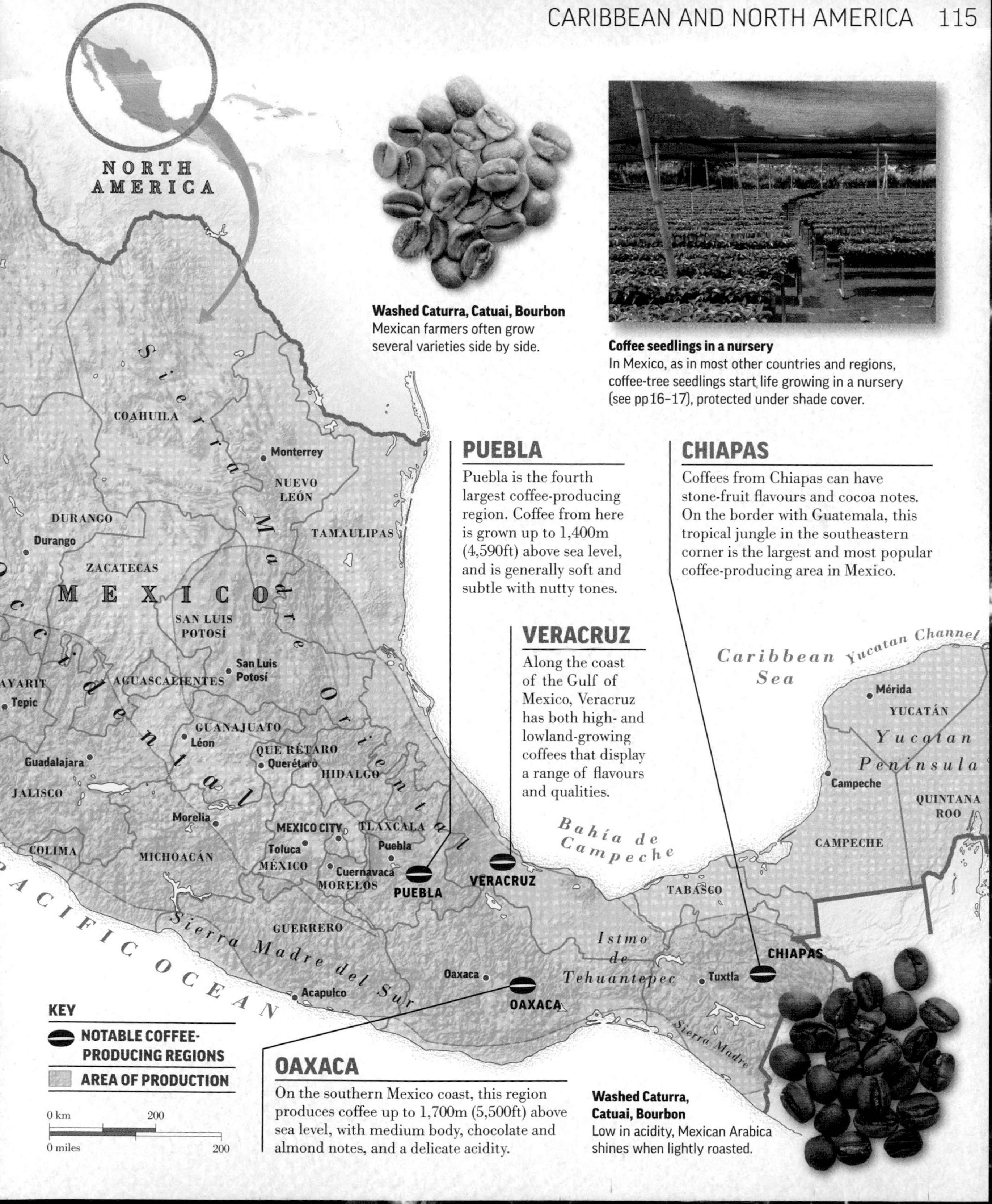

PUEBLA

Puebla is the fourth
largest coffee-producing
region. Coffee from here
is grown up to 1,400m
(4,590ft) above sea level,
and is generally soft and
subtle with nutty tones.

CHIAPAS

Coffees from Chiapas can have
stone-fruit flavours and cocoa notes.
On the border with Guatemala, this
tropical jungle in the southeastern
corner is the largest and most popular
coffee-producing area in Mexico.

VERACRUZ

Along the coast
of the Gulf of
Mexico, Veracruz
has both high- and
lowland-growing
coffees that display
a range of flavours
and qualities.

OAXACA

On the southern Mexico coast, this region
produces coffee up to 1,700m (5,500ft) above
sea level, with medium body, chocolate and
almond notes, and a delicate acidity.

**Washed Caturra,
Catuai, Bourbon**
Low in acidity, Mexican Arabica
shines when lightly roasted.

KEY

⬛ NOTABLE COFFEE-
PRODUCING REGIONS

▨ AREA OF PRODUCTION

0 km   200

0 miles   200

PUERTO RICO

NORTH AMERICA

One of the smallest coffee-producing nations, Puerto Rico grows sweet, low-acidity coffees with a smooth, rounded texture and cedar, herbal, and almond notes.

Coffee production in Puerto Rico has declined in recent years due to political instability, climate change, and high production costs. It is estimated that nearly half of the crop is left unharvested due to a lack of pickers.

Farms are located throughout the western central mountains from Rincon to Orocovis, with most of the coffee grown at 750–850m (2,460–2,780ft) above sea level. However, there is also potential for growing at higher altitudes, such as in Ponce, where the highest peak reaches 1,338m (4,390ft) above sea level.

Arabica varieties are mainly grown here, including Bourbon, Typica, Pacas, and Catimor. Puerto Ricans drink only a third of the homegrown coffee – the rest comes from the Dominican Republic and Mexico. A small quantity is exported.

JAYUYA

Also known as the indigenous capital of the country, nestled in the tropical cloud forests in the Cordillera Central, Jayuya has the second highest altitude in Puerto Rico.

ADJUNTAS

Mediterranean immigrants brought coffee to this area, which is nicknamed the "Switzerland of Puerto Rico" for its cool climate and altitudes of up to 1,000m (3,280ft) above sea level.

LAS MARIAS

Known as the City of Citrus Fruit, Las Marias' agriculture also centres around coffee. Many of the old coffee haciendas are on the route of the Puerto Rican coffee tour operators.

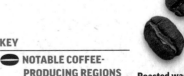

Washed Pacas
Imported from El Salvador, the Pacas grows successfully on Puerto Rican soil.

PUERTO RICAN COFFEE

PERCENTAGE OF WORLD MARKET:	**LESS THAN 0.01%**
HARVEST:	**AUGUST–MARCH**
PROCESS:	**WASHED**

MAIN TYPES:
ARABICA
BOURBON, TYPICA, CATURRA, CATUAI, PACAS, SARCHIMOR LIMANI, CATIMOR PEDIMENT

WORLD RANKING AS A PRODUCER: **52ND LARGEST PRODUCER IN THE WORLD**

KEY

 **NOTABLE COFFEE-PRODUCING REGIONS**

AREA OF PRODUCTION

0 km   30
0 miles   30

Roasted washed Catimor
A hybrid of Robusta and Arabica, Catimors grow and yield well in most areas, Puerto Rico being no exception.

HAWAII

Hawaiian coffees are balanced, clean, delicate, and mild with some milk chocolate, subtle fruity acidity, and medium body. They can be aromatic and sweet.

Hawaii mainly grows varieties of Arabica, such as Typica, Catuai and Caturra. Hawaiian coffees are well-marketed and expensive, which means they are some of the most counterfeited coffees in the world – especially the coffee from Kona.

On the island, coffee has to have at least 10 per cent Kona-grown coffee beans in it to bear the name, while, controversially, mainland US has no such rules.

Production and labour cost is high; many stages are highly mechanized.

COFFEE INTERCROPPING
Growers are increasingly planting other trees alongside the coffee trees to help to provide shade.

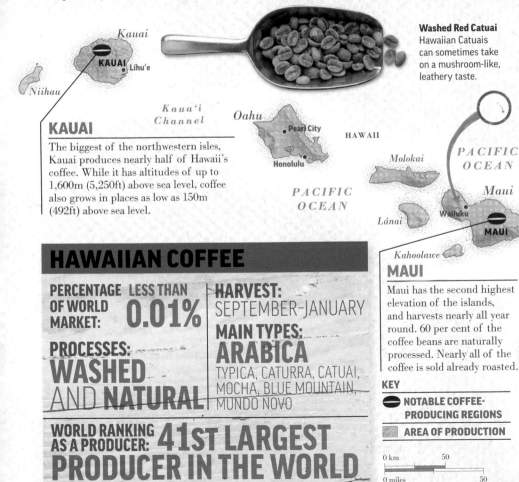

Washed Red Catuai
Hawaiian Catuais can sometimes take on a mushroom-like, leathery taste.

NORTH AMERICA

KAUAI
The biggest of the northwestern isles, Kauai produces nearly half of Hawaii's coffee. While it has altitudes of up to 1,600m (5,250ft) above sea level, coffee also grows in places as low as 150m (492ft) above sea level.

MAUI
Maui has the second highest elevation of the islands, and harvests nearly all year round. 60 per cent of the coffee beans are naturally processed. Nearly all of the coffee is sold already roasted.

HAWAII
The areas of Kona, Ka'u, Hamakua, and North Hilo stretch down the sides of the Mauna Loa volcano, and the coffee trees here thrive in the rich, black soil. Most of the coffees from this island are fully washed.

KEY

 NOTABLE COFFEE-PRODUCING REGIONS

AREA OF PRODUCTION

0 km   50
0 miles   50

Kauai · KAUAI · Lihu'e · *Niihau* · *Kaua'i Channel* · *Oahu* · Pearl City · HAWAII · Honolulu · *PACIFIC OCEAN* · *Molokai* · *PACIFIC OCEAN* · *Maui* · Wailuku · MAUI · *Lánai* · *Kahoolawe* · Hilo · HAWAII · *Hawaii*

HAWAIIAN COFFEE

PERCENTAGE OF WORLD MARKET: LESS THAN **0.01%**

HARVEST: SEPTEMBER–JANUARY

MAIN TYPES: ARABICA TYPICA, CATURRA, CATUAI, MOCHA, BLUE MOUNTAIN, MUNDO NOVO

PROCESSES: WASHED AND NATURAL

WORLD RANKING AS A PRODUCER: 41ST LARGEST PRODUCER IN THE WORLD

FLAVOUR PAIRINGS

**You can pair coffee with complementary flavours
to create exciting drinks. Try sweet, rich, fresh, or
spicy pairings, for results that will surprise your palate.**

Berries
Raspberry, cherry,
strawberry, and huckleberry.
For a creamy berry-flavoured
coffee, try **Strawberry
lace** (p180).

Nuts
Pistachio, peanut,
hazelnut, almond, cashew,
chestnut, walnut, and
pecan. The **Almond
affogato** (p178) is topped
with chopped almonds.

Drinks
Darjeeling tea, brandy,
beer, cognac, whisky,
Cointreau, rum, gin, and
tequila. The classic
alcoholic coffee, **Irish
coffee** (p208) marries the
flavours of whisky and
coffee perfectly.

Herbs
Rosemary, sage, eucalyptus,
tarragon, basil, peppermint,
coriander, hops, chamomile,
elderflower, and bergamot.
Breath of fresh air
(p195) pairs coffee
with peppermint.

Dairy
Milk, milk substitutes
such as soya, almond,
or rice milk, cream,
yogurt, and butter. For a
dairy-free option, try **Rice
milk ice latte** (p192).

SPICY · FRUITY · CARAMEL

Exotic fruits
Mango, lychee, pineapple, and coconut. For a hot, delicious drink, coconut lovers can try *Mochi affogato* (p177).

Orchard fruits
Apple, pear, and fig. For a hot black coffee with an apple–berry twist, try *I'm your huckleberry* (p168).

Citrus
Lemon and orange. Lemon juice adds freshness to a glass of cold-brewed coffee such as *Caribbean punch* (p190).

Stone fruits
Apricot and nectarine. For a refreshing cold coffee, try *Apricot star* (p193).

Syrups and sweeteners
Honey, molasses, cocoa powder, and caramel. For a naturally sweetened cold coffee, try *Milk and honey* (p199).

Spices
Chilli, vanilla, ginger, lemongrass, cinnamon, liquorice, nutmeg, saffron, and cumin. Try *Syphon spice* (p172) for coffee infused with nutmeg.

JAMAICA

Some of the most well-marketed and expensive coffees in the world grow here. Beans are sweet, soft, and mellow, with nutty notes and medium textures.

The most famous Jamaican coffees are those from the Blue Mountain range. These iconic beans ship in wooden barrels rather than jute or burlap bags. The variety is expensive, but often counterfeit – either partially or completely – and measures are being developed to protect it. Typica also grows here in large quantities.

BLUE MOUNTAIN PLANTATION
A Jamaican coffee estate on the slopes of the Blue Mountain, with mineral-rich, fertile soil.

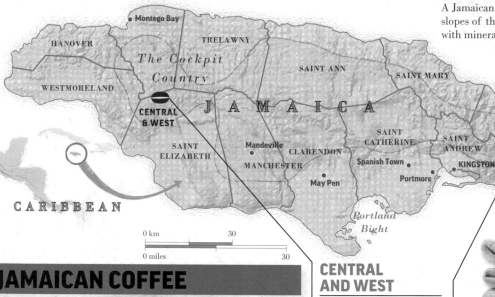

JAMAICAN COFFEE

PERCENTAGE OF WORLD MARKET:	LESS THAN **0.01%**	**HARVEST: SEPTEMBER–MARCH**
MAIN TYPES: ARABICA MOSTLY TYPICA, BLUE MOUNTAIN		**PROCESS:** WASHED

WORLD RANKING AS A PRODUCER: 44TH LARGEST COFFEE PRODUCER IN THE WORLD

CENTRAL AND WEST

While they are not named Blue Mountain, the rest of Jamaica grows the same variety, but in different microclimates and at lower altitudes, peaking at around 1,000m (3,280ft) above sea level where the borders of Trelawny, Manchester, Clarendon, and Saint Ann meet.

KEY

⬬ **NOTABLE COFFEE-PRODUCING REGIONS**

▨ **AREA OF PRODUCTION**

Washed Typica and Catuai
Typica is widely cultivated, whereas Catuai is a newer variety to Jamaica.

EAST

The Blue Mountain peaks at 2,256m (7,400ft) and borders Portland and Saint Thomas. The mountain range provides a cool, misty climate, well-suited to coffee growing.

DOMINICAN REPUBLIC

There are several growing regions here with varying microclimates. They produce coffee that ranges from chocolatey, spicy, and heavy to floral, bright, and delicate.

As many Dominicans drink local coffee, only a modest amount is exported. Combined with low prices and hurricane damage, this has led to a decline in quality. Most coffee is Arabica – Typica, Caturra, and Catuai. Measures are being taken to improve the coffee grown here.

HARVEST SEASON
Harvest runs almost all year round, due to lack of a consistent climate or defined wet season.

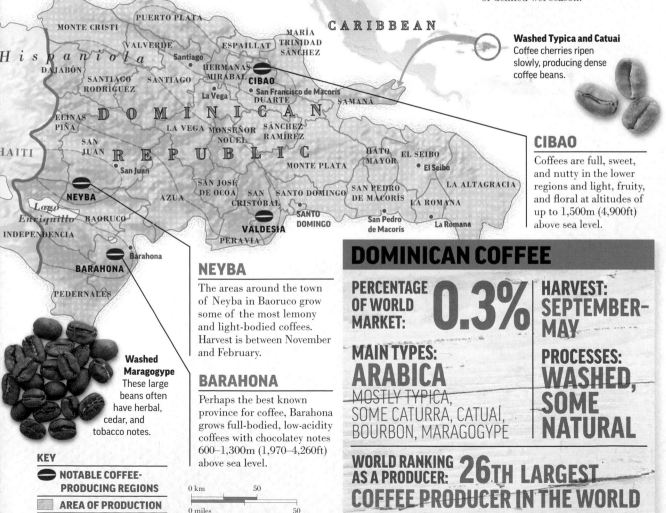

Washed Typica and Catuai
Coffee cherries ripen slowly, producing dense coffee beans.

CIBAO
Coffees are full, sweet, and nutty in the lower regions and light, fruity, and floral at altitudes of up to 1,500m (4,900ft) above sea level.

NEYBA
The areas around the town of Neyba in Baoruco grow some of the most lemony and light-bodied coffees. Harvest is between November and February.

BARAHONA
Perhaps the best known province for coffee, Barahona grows full-bodied, low-acidity coffees with chocolatey notes 600–1,300m (1,970–4,260ft) above sea level.

Washed Maragogype
These large beans often have herbal, cedar, and tobacco notes.

KEY
- ⬤ NOTABLE COFFEE-PRODUCING REGIONS
- ▢ AREA OF PRODUCTION

0 km   50
0 miles   50

DOMINICAN COFFEE

PERCENTAGE OF WORLD MARKET: **0.3%**

HARVEST: SEPTEMBER–MAY

MAIN TYPES: ARABICA
MOSTLY TYPICA, SOME CATURRA, CATUAÍ, BOURBON, MARAGOGYPE

PROCESSES: WASHED, SOME NATURAL

WORLD RANKING AS A PRODUCER: 26TH LARGEST COFFEE PRODUCER IN THE WORLD

CUBA

Cuban coffees have a mixed reputation and are highly priced. They are generally heavy-bodied, with low acidity, balanced sweetness, and earthy tobacco notes.

Coffee was introduced to Cuba in the mid-1700s. Cuba grew to become one of the world's largest exporters before political turmoil and economic restrictions saw it surpassed by South American countries. The majority of the crop is Arabica – Villalobos and Isla 6–14. Cubans drink more coffee than they grow, so only a minor percentage is exported. Only a small part of the island has the altitude to grow speciality grades, but the mineral-rich soil and climate increases its potential.

CUBAN MOUNTAIN RANGES
Steep Cuban mountain ranges provide a cool climate with good sun exposure.

Washed Villalobos
The sweetness of this variety can balance the rustic notes that local microclimates promote.

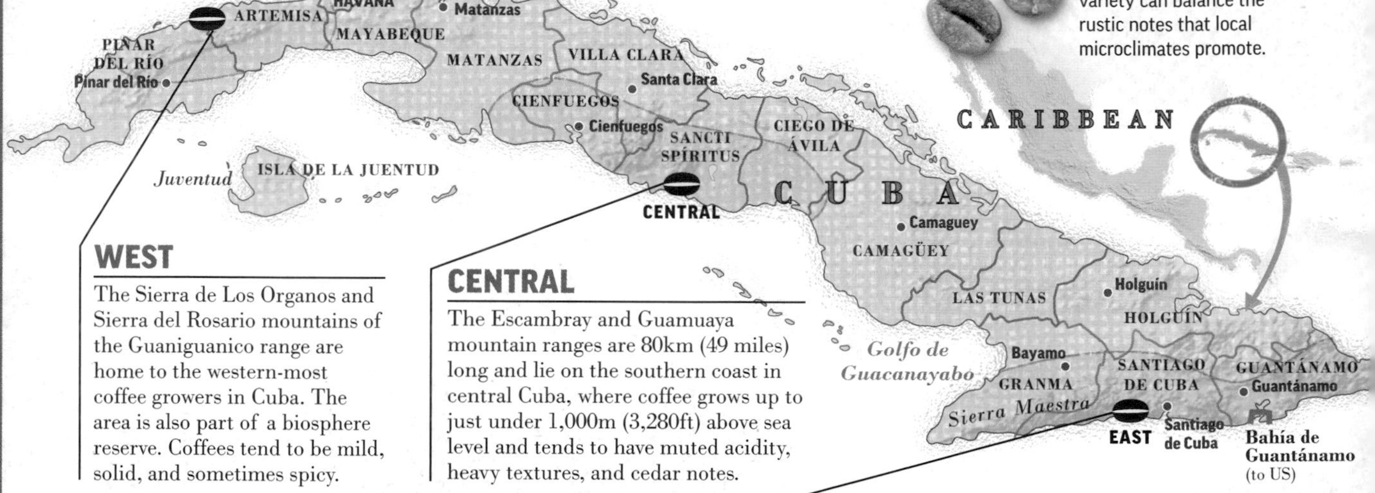

WEST

The Sierra de Los Organos and Sierra del Rosario mountains of the Guaniguanico range are home to the western-most coffee growers in Cuba. The area is also part of a biosphere reserve. Coffees tend to be mild, solid, and sometimes spicy.

CENTRAL

The Escambray and Guamuaya mountain ranges are 80km (49 miles) long and lie on the southern coast in central Cuba, where coffee grows up to just under 1,000m (3,280ft) above sea level and tends to have muted acidity, heavy textures, and cedar notes.

EAST

The Sierra Maestra and Sierra Cristal are mountains along the southern coast of the east of Cuba. This area has the highest altitudes, with Turquino Peak rising up to 1,974m (6,200ft) above sea level – the best climate for more complex speciality coffee.

Washed Bourbon
In local tradition, Cuban coffees are often roasted to quite a dark level.

CUBAN COFFEE KEY FACTS

PERCENTAGE OF WORLD MARKET:	LESS THAN 0.1%	MAIN TYPE: ARABICA VILLALOBOS, ISLA 6-14 SOME ROBUSTA	HARVEST: JULY–FEBRUARY
PROCESSES: WASHED			

WORLD RANKING AS A PRODUCER: 40TH LARGEST PRODUCER

KEY

⬤ NOTABLE COFFEE-PRODUCING REGIONS

▨ AREA OF PRODUCTION

Map labels: HAVANA, HAVANA, ARTEMISA, WEST, Matanzas, MAYABEQUE, MATANZAS, PINAR DEL RÍO, Pinar del Río, VILLA CLARA, Santa Clara, CIENFUEGOS, Cienfuegos, SANCTI SPÍRITUS, CIEGO DE ÁVILA, CARIBBEAN, Juventud, ISLA DE LA JUENTUD, CENTRAL, CUBA, Camaguey, CAMAGÜEY, LAS TUNAS, Holguín, HOLGUÍN, Golfo de Guacanayabo, Bayamo, GRANMA, Sierra Maestra, SANTIAGO DE CUBA, GUANTÁNAMO, Guantánamo, EAST, Santiago de Cuba, Bahía de Guantánamo (to US)

0 km 150
0 miles 150

HAITI

Most coffees from Haiti are naturally processed and nutty with fruity tones. Washed coffees with sweet and citrus notes are on the rise.

Coffee has been grown in Haiti since 1725. The country was once responsible for half of the world's production. Hindered by political turmoil and natural disasters, there are now few coffee-growing areas and skilled smallholders. A very high internal consumption adds to these challenges. However, with altitudes of 2,000m (6,560ft) and heavily shaded forest, the coffee industry has great potential. Haiti grows Arabica varieties, such as Typica, Bourbon, and Caturra.

CARIBBEAN

Tortue

Port-de-Paix

NORD-OUEST

Cap-Haïtien

Hispaniola

NORD

NORD-EST

Gonaïves

ARTIBONITE

Hinche

H A I T I

DOMINICAN REPUBLIC

Gonâve

Washed Bourbon
When lightly roasted, Bourbon beans are sweet with subtle stone-fruit notes.

CENTRE

Lake Azuei

PORT-AU-PRINCE

OUEST

ARTIBONITE AND CENTRE

While these areas do not grow as much as the Nord department, the Belladere, Savanette, and Petite Riviere de l'Artibonite communes have a lot of potential for growth.

Jérémie

GRAND'ANSE

Massif de la Hotte

NIPPES

SOUTH

SOUTHEAST

Jacmel

Cayes

Vache

GRAND'ANSE

This easternmost region is home to a majority of the 175,000 families who grow coffee in Haiti, most of them with small farms with up to 7 hectares (17 acres) each.

Washed Villalobos
Haitian coffees tend to be naturals, but varieties like the Villalobos really shine when washed.

SOUTH AND SOUTHEAST

Haiti's southern coast – particularly the area bordering Dominican Republic – is home to many of the smallest farms with conditions suitable for growing high-quality coffee.

KEY

⬤ **NOTABLE COFFEE-PRODUCING REGIONS**

▨ **AREA OF PRODUCTION**

0 km   50
0 miles   50

HAITIAN COFFEE KEY FACTS

PERCENTAGE OF WORLD MARKET: **0.2%**

PROCESSES: NATURAL, SOME WASHED

HARVEST: AUGUST–MARCH

MAIN TYPES: ARABICA TYPICA, BOURBON, CATURRA, CATIMOR, VILLALOBOS

WORLD RANKING AS A PRODUCER: **30TH LARGEST PRODUCER**

EQUIPMENT

ESPRESSO MACHINE

An espresso machine relies on pump pressure to force water through coffee to extract the desired solubles. It produces a small and viscous drink when used correctly – an intense shot that is balanced between sweet and acidic. The technique for using the machine is shown on pages 42–47.

Warming time
A standard machine takes about 20–30 minutes to heat up to the correct temperature, so keep this in mind before you brew.

WHAT YOU NEED

• **Fine ground coffee** (see p39)

The tamper
Use this to compress the bed of coffee down to expel pockets of air and create a compact, even layer of grounds. This layer needs to withstand the pressure of water and allow all the coffee to extract as uniformly as possible. A rubber tamping mat will protect your table from getting dented by the spouts.

The filter basket
The coffee is portioned into a removable filter basket held in place with a clip. Baskets come in a range of sizes depending on how much coffee you prefer to use when preparing your espresso. The number, shape, and size of the tiny holes at the bottom of the basket will also impact the result you get in the cup.

Portafilter
The filter basket fits into a portafilter, which is a handle with one or two spouts.

Pressure gauge
Many home espresso machines are advertised as having unnecessarily high bar pressure. Professional machines are normally set to brew at 9 bars, with a steam pressure of 1-1.5 bars. Some machines will have the option of allowing pre-infusion, an initial phase of gently wetting the coffee before full pump pressure is applied.

Water temperature
Adjust this to 90-95°C (195-200°F) – this should bring out the best flavours in the coffee. Some coffees taste better with hot water, others better with cooler water.

The group head
The portafilter fastens into a group head where water is dispersed through a metal screen onto the bed of coffee, saturating and extracting it evenly.

The boilers
The machines will generally have one or two boilers inside, providing and heating up the water used for brewing, creating the steam used to steam milk, and a separate hot water tap for miscellaneous use.

The steam arm
The steam arm should be movable to allow you to set it at an angle that works for you. The steam tips or nozzles come in various options that allow you to choose the force and direction of steam that you enjoy working with. Keep this clean at all times, as milk quickly bakes on both the inside and outside of the steam wand.

FRENCH PRESS

The classic press, sometimes known as a cafetière, is a great vessel for brewing good coffee. It's simple and quick – water and coffee infuse together before a mesh filter pushes through the brew, leaving oils and fine particles. This gives the coffee a great texture.

WHAT YOU NEED

- **Medium–coarse ground coffee** (see p39)
- **Digital weighing scale** to help get the coffee–water ratio right.

HOW IT WORKS

❶ **Preheat** the press with hot water then discard the water. Place the press on a scale and tare.

❷ **Add the coffee** to the press and tare again. A good ratio to start with is 30g (1oz) coffee to 500ml (16fl oz) water.

❸ **Add the water,** checking it is the right volume and temperature, preferably 90-94°C (195-200°F).

❹ **Stir the coffee** once or twice.

❺ **Leave to brew** for 4 minutes, then carefully stir the surface again.

❻ **Skim** the foam and floating particles off the surface with a spoon.

❼ **Place the filter** on top of the press and gently push down until the grounds are collected at the bottom. If you meet too much resistance, you may have used too much coffee, too fine a grind, or not let the coffee steep for long enough.

❽ **Allow to rest** in the press for a couple of minutes, then serve.

CLEANING

- **Often dishwasher safe** Check your model.
- **Dismantle** This avoids trapped grounds and oils that may impart a bitter or sour flavour.

Plunger
This plunger pushes the mesh filter through the brew, and separates and retains the grounds at the bottom of the pot.

Brew time
Brew for 4 minutes. After plunging, allow the press to rest for 2 minutes more to allow particles to settle before you pour.

Mesh filter
Unscrew each element of this after you've served (see Cleaning, left).

Stir twice
Stir before brewing to saturate the grounds, then after to settle them.

FILTER POUR-OVER

Brewing through a paper filter is an easy way to make coffee straight into a mug or serving vessel. As the grounds are easily disposed of with the paper filter, the method is also clean and stress-free.

WHAT YOU NEED

- **Medium ground coffee** (see p39)
- **Digital weighing scale** to help you get the coffee–water ratio right.

HOW IT WORKS

1 **Rinse** the paper filter well. Preheat the filter holder and jug or mug with warm water. Discard the water.

2 **Place the jug** or mug onto a scale. Place the filter on top, and tare.

3 **Add the coffee** to the filter and tare again. A good ratio to start with is 60g (2oz) coffee to 1 litre (1¾ pints) water.

4 **Saturate the grounds** with a little water at preferably 90–94°C (195–200°F), and leave them to swell for about 30 seconds to allow the "bloom" to settle.

5 **Keep pouring water** over in a slow, continuous stream or in portions until you have poured over the right volume of water. Serve when the water has filtered through.

CLEANING

- **Dishwasher safe** Most filter holders are machine washable.
- **Sponge wash** Use a soft sponge and some lightly soapy water to rinse off any oils and particles.

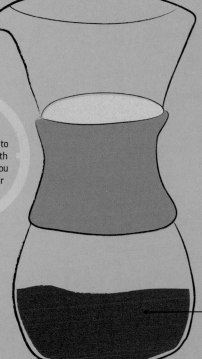

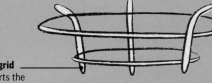

Paper filter
These hold back fine particles and oil. While they can impart some flavour to the brew, choosing bleached filters and rinsing them well helps to reduce the paper-like taste.

Filter holder
This sits on top of your jug or serving vessel.

Pouring water
Keep the coffee submerged when you pour over the water, or let it build up along the sides of the filter as the water flows through the centre – see what works for you.

Filter grid
Supports the filter in the holder.

Brew time
It should take 3–4 minutes for the water to filter through. Play with grind and dose until you get a time and flavour that you like.

Serving jug
Brew into a jug or directly into a cup.

CLOTH BREWER

A traditional way of filtering through the grounds, cloth-brewing is also known as "sock" or "nel" brewing. Fans prefer it to paper-filter brewing because the process doesn't impart a papery flavour. The coffee also gains a richer texture due to the oils that pass through the cloth.

WHAT YOU NEED

- **Medium ground coffee** (see p39)
- **Digital weighing scale** to help you get the coffee–water ratio right.

HOW IT WORKS

❶ **Rinse** the cloth filter thoroughly in hot water before the first use to clean and preheat the filter. If you have frozen your filter (see below), this process will defrost it at the same time.

❷ **Place the filter** on top of the brewing vessel and pour hot water through to preheat it. Discard the water.

❸ **Tare the brewer** by placing it on a digital scale.

❹ **Add the coffee,** working on a base recipe of 15g (½oz) coffee to 250ml (9oz) water.

❺ **Wet the grounds** with a little water at approximately 90–94℃ (195–200°F). Let them swell for 30–45 seconds to allow the "bloom" to settle down.

❻ **Continue pouring water** over the coffee in a gentle, continuous stream or in stages. When all the water has filtered through, serve the coffee.

CLEANING

- **Reusable** Discard the grounds and rinse filters in hot water. Do not use soap.
- **Keep moist** Either freeze filters when wet or keep in a sealed container in the fridge.

Pouring water
Try not to overfill the filter when you pour the water over the coffee grounds. Instead, pour it at a gentle speed so that the filter is never more than three-quarters full.

Cloth filter

Filter function
As the water is poured over the coffee, the cloth holds back the fine coffee particles.

Brew time
The water should take 3–4 minutes to filter through. Play with the grind and dose until you get the right time and flavour.

Serving jug

AEROPRESS

A quick and clean brewer, an AeroPress can brew a full filter-style cup, or a strong, more concentrated coffee that can be diluted with hot water. It is easy to play with grind, dose of coffee, and pressure, making it a wonderfully flexible choice.

WHAT YOU NEED

- **Fine–medium ground coffee** (see p39)
- **Digital weighing scale** to help you get the coffee–water ratio right.

HOW IT WORKS

1. **Insert the plunger** about 2cm (³⁄₄in) into the brew chamber.
2. **Tare the AeroPress** by placing it on a scale, inverted, plunger down and brew chamber up. Ensure the seal is tight and stable and that the AeroPress will not fall over.
3. **Add 12g (¼oz) coffee** to the brew chamber and tare the brewer again.
4. **Add 200ml (7fl oz) hot water** and stir carefully to avoid knocking the AeroPress over. Let sit for 30–60 seconds and stir again.
5. **Place a filter paper** in the cap and rinse it well, then screw it onto the brew chamber.
6. **Quickly but gently flip** the AeroPress over to sit filter cap down on top of a sturdy cup or serving vessel.
7. **Press the plunger down** gently to brew the coffee into your cup. Serve.

CLEANING

- **Taking apart** Twist off the filter cap and push the plunger all the way through to pop out the spent grounds in the filter. Discard.
- **Wash** Rinse well and use soapy water, or wash in the dishwasher.

ALTERNATIVE METHOD

Rather than flipping the AeroPress over the cup at step 6, place the empty AeroPress (with filter paper in the cap) over the vessel. Add coffee and water. As soon as the coffee and water are poured in, the plunger needs to be quickly placed on top to keep the coffee from dripping into the cup.

Plunger
This sits inside the brew chamber and is used to push the coffee through the filter cap.

Brew chamber
The coffee and water in the brew chamber is compressed through a filter by the plunger.

Filter cap
The paper filter sits in the filter cap and is screwed to the brew chamber.

SYPHON

One of the most visually interesting methods of brewing coffee, syphons are particularly popular in Japan. Brewing takes time in a syphon, but this is part of its ceremonial appeal.

WHAT YOU NEED

- **Medium ground coffee** (see p39)

HOW IT WORKS

❶ Fill the bottom bowl of the syphon with near-boiling water, up to the desired number of cups.

❷ Position the filter in the brew chamber by dropping it in and pulling the beaded string through the funnel until the little hook can fasten to the opening. The string should touch the glass of the bowl.

❸ Place the funnel gently into the bowl of water. Rest the chamber on a slight slant without sealing the bowl off.

❹ Light the flame, and as the water starts to boil, secure the brew chamber onto the bowl. Don't tighten it, just ensure it is sealed. The brew chamber will begin to fill. Some water remains in the bowl below the funnel.

❺ When the brew chamber has filled, add the coffee – 15g (¹/₂oz) coffee to 250ml (9fl oz) water – and stir for a few seconds.

❻ Allow to brew for one minute.

❼ Stir the coffee again and remove the flame to begin the draw down process.

❽ When the coffee has drained into the bottom bowl, gently remove the brew chamber and serve.

CLEANING

- **Paper filter** Discard this and rinse the filter holder in soapy water.
- **Cloth filter** Use the technique on p130.

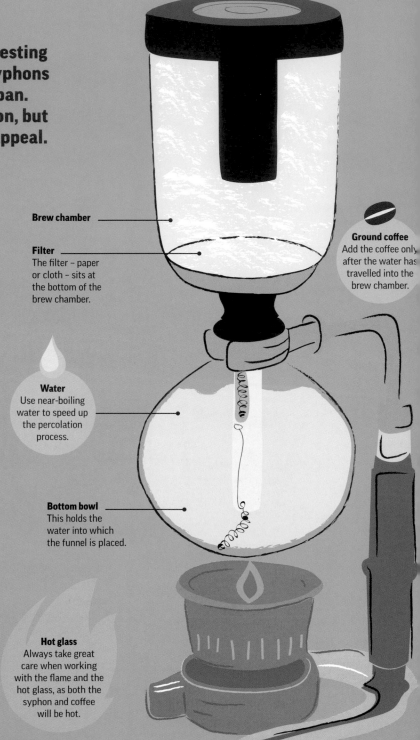

Brew chamber

Filter
The filter – paper or cloth – sits at the bottom of the brew chamber.

Ground coffee
Add the coffee only after the water has travelled into the brew chamber.

Water
Use near-boiling water to speed up the percolation process.

Bottom bowl
This holds the water into which the funnel is placed.

Hot glass
Always take great care when working with the flame and the hot glass, as both the syphon and coffee will be hot.

STOVE-TOP POT

The stove-top, or moka pot, brews a strong cup of coffee using steam pressure, which imparts a silky texture. Contrary to popular belief, it is not designed to make espresso, but its use of high temperatures gives the coffee an intense flavour.

WHAT YOU NEED

- **Medium ground coffee** (see p39)

HOW IT WORKS

1. **Pour hot water** into the bottom pot until it is just under the inside valve.
2. **Fill the filter with coffee** loosely, following a ratio of 25g (scant 1oz) coffee to 500ml (16fl oz) water. Level it off.
3. **Place the filter** in the bottom pot and screw on the top section.
4. **Place the stove-top pot** over a medium heat, leaving the lid open.
5. **Monitor the brew** as the water boils and coffee begins to appear.
6. **Remove the pot from the heat** when the coffee goes pale in colour and starts to bubble.
7. **Wait until the bubbling stops**, then serve.

CLEANING

- **Allow to cool** Let the pot sit for 30 minutes before dismantling it, or run it under cold water to cool it down.
- **Sponge in hot water** Do not clean the parts with soap. Using a non-abrasive sponge or brush and hot water will be sufficient.

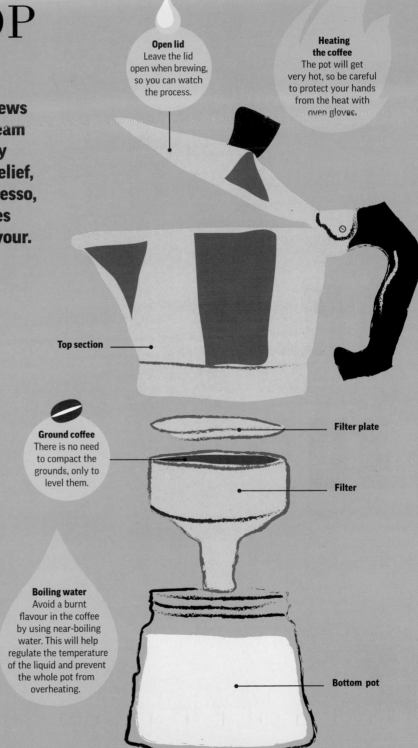

Open lid
Leave the lid open when brewing, so you can watch the process.

Heating the coffee
The pot will get very hot, so be careful to protect your hands from the heat with oven gloves.

Top section

Ground coffee
There is no need to compact the grounds, only to level them.

Filter plate

Filter

Boiling water
Avoid a burnt flavour in the coffee by using near-boiling water. This will help regulate the temperature of the liquid and prevent the whole pot from overheating.

Bottom pot

COLD DRIPPER

Use cold water to brew low-acidity coffee that can be served cold or hot. It is not as easy to extract with cold water, so it requires more time and a cold dripper tower. If you don't have one, you can also add the coffee and water to a French press, leave it overnight in the fridge, then strain it through a filter.

WHAT YOU NEED

- **Medium ground coffee** (see p39)

HOW IT WORKS

❶ **Close the drip valve** on the top chamber and fill it with cold water.

❷ **Rinse the middle chamber filter** thoroughly, and add the coffee. Use a ratio of 60g (2oz) coffee to 500ml (16fl oz) water.

❸ **Shake gently to distribute** evenly, and cover with another rinsed filter.

❹ **Open the valve** and allow a small amount of water to run into the coffee to wet it and start the extraction.

❺ **Adjust the valve** to drip about once every two seconds, or 30–40 drops per minute.

❻ **When all the water** has dripped through, you will have cold coffee you can enjoy neat, diluted with hot or cold water, or served over ice.

CLEANING

- **Hand wash** Follow the manufacturer's instructions. If in doubt, wash gently with hot water and a soft cloth, without soap. Rinse the cloth filter in water and store it in the fridge or freezer between uses.

Cold water
The cold water slowly drips through during the brew process.

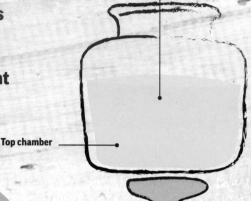

Top chamber

Brew time
It should take around 5–6 hours for 500ml (16fl oz) of brewed coffee to filter through the cold dripper tower.

Middle chamber

Filter

BREWING DOUBLE-STRENGTH

Another way to produce cold-brewed coffee is to brew it double-strength over ice using a filter pour-over, cloth brewer, or AeroPress. Use 60g (2oz) coffee and 500ml (16fl oz) hot water. Fill a serving vessel with ice cubes; while brewing, the ice will chill and dilute the coffee to the right temperature and strength. Note that this method will bring out acids and compounds from the coffee not extracted with a cold dripper.

ELECTRIC FILTER-BREW

This humble coffee maker may not seem like an exciting way to brew, but it can produce great coffee if you use quality beans and fresh water. It is easy to clean, as the grounds are easily removed and composted.

WHAT YOU NEED

- **Medium ground coffee** (see p39)
- **Pre-heated thermos** to store leftover coffee.

HOW IT WORKS

❶ **Fill the reservoir** of the machine with fresh, cold water.

❷ **Rinse the paper filter** thoroughly and place it in its holder.

❸ **Add coffee** measuring about 60g (2oz) coffee to 1 litre (1¾ pints) water and shake the filter holder gently to distribute.

❹ **Place the filter** back in the machine and start the brew cycle. When the machine has finished brewing, serve.

CLEANING

- **Use filtered water** This reduces limescale build-up and helps to keep the heating element and water lines clear.
- **Descaling** A descaling solution can be a good preventative measure against limescale build-up.

Brew time
It should take about 4–5 minutes. If you have brewed too much coffee, decant the leftover into a pre-heated thermos.

Filter

Serving jug

Fresh water
Filtered or bottled water prevents scaling and imparts a fresh flavour.

PHIN

Easy to use, the Vietnamese phin uses a gravity-based filter insert to compress the coffee. In Chinese phins, the filter is screwed on, allowing more extraction control. All phins are very user-friendly, enabling you to change grind and dose to your preference.

WHAT YOU NEED

- **Fine–medium ground coffee** (see p39)

HOW IT WORKS

1 **Preheat** the phin by placing the phin saucer and the phin cup on top of a mug, and pouring hot water through. Discard the water from the mug.

2 **Place the coffee** in the bottom of the phin cup – use a ratio of 7g (a heaped teaspoon) coffee to 100ml (3½fl oz) water – and shake gently to distribute the coffee grounds evenly.

3 **Place the filter** on top, twisting it a little to even out the grounds.

4 **Pour** about one-third of the hot water over the filter. Allow the coffee to swell for 1 minute.

5 **Continue to pour** the rest of the water over the filter. Place the lid on the phin to retain the heat, and watch as the water slowly drips through to brew the coffee. After 4–5 minutes, serve your drink.

CLEANING

- **Dishwasher** Most can be washed in the dishwasher, but check your instructions.
- **Easy cleaning** Hot water and soap are also fine for removing coffee oils from the metal cup and filter.

Brew time
The water should drip through in about 4–5 minutes. If it takes less or more time, adjust the grind or dose to suit.

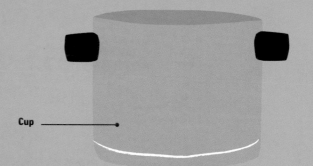

Lid
The lid helps retain heat during brewing and is used as a saucer to catch any drips after brewing.

Filter

Cup

Saucer

Mug

IBRIK

Popular in Eastern Europe and the Middle East, the ibrik, also known as cezve, briki, rakwa, finjan, and kanaka, is a tin-lined copper pot with a long handle. It brews coffee with a distinct, thick texture. The superfine grind, amount of heat, and grind-water ratio produces a full-flavoured coffee.

WHAT YOU NEED

- **Very fine, powder-like coffee** (see p39)

HOW IT WORKS

1. **Pour cold water** into the ibrik, and bring it to the boil over a medium heat.
2. **Remove** from the heat.
3. **Add coffee** to the ibrik – 1 teaspoon per cup – and any additional ingredients, if desired.
4. **Stir to dissolve** and infuse the ingredients.
5. **Return the ibrik** to the stove and heat the coffee while stirring gently until it starts foaming. Do not allow to boil.
6. **Remove from the heat** and allow to cool for 1 minute.
7. **Return to the heat** and warm back up while stirring gently until it starts foaming. Again do not allow to boil. Repeat this.
8. **Spoon a little foam** into the serving cups and carefully pour the coffee in.
9. **Let it settle** for a couple of minutes, and serve. Take care to stop sipping when you reach the grounds in the bottom of the cup.

CLEANING

- **Sponging** Use a non-abrasive sponge or soft brush with some hot soapy water to hand wash the ibrik.
- **Care** The tin lining might darken over time. This is normal so do not attempt to remove it.

Repeated heating
You can heat the coffee once, if you prefer, but reheating it several times creates the distinctive thick texture.

Handle
The long handle requires some precision. When pouring the coffee into the cup, pour slowly so that the foam does not collapse.

Brew chamber
It is traditional to mix sugar and spices with the ground coffee. See recipe, p169.

SERVING VESSELS

The texture, shape, size, and design of the vessel you serve coffee in can affect your drinking experience. Many argue that certain cups, glasses, and mugs must be used for certain recipes – but it often comes down to personal preference.

While some cups were designed to enhance the presentation of the beverage, such as the espresso cup, others were designed with a more practical purpose in mind. For instance, the first American diner mugs were thick enough to retain heat for a long time, rough at the bottom so they would not slide around on the table, and nearly indestructible, making them perfect for use by the military during World War II.

Design aside, it is fun to try out different drinking vessels from time to time, to enhance both the presentation and experience.

Small porcelain tumbler
Cups without handles have a modern appeal. Some prefer the comfort of a thicker rim when drinking espresso. It is also perfect for many small-volume coffee beverages.

Espresso glass
The visual appeal of espresso – with its dark liquid and golden brown crema – presents itself beautifully in a glass. It also retains heat well, but take care, as it may become quite hot to touch.

Demitasse espresso cup
A soft, rounded interior allows the crema to land gently and retain its texture, heat, and visual appeal.

Large cup
Sometimes it is okay to want a big cup of coffee – just choose a ceramic one that is insulating enough to keep your beverage warm.

Earthenware cup
Many like the sensory experience of earthenware on their lips. The material also retains heat well.

Large mug
The good old-fashioned diner mug feels heavy and comforting in the hand. A thick edge feels softer on the lips than a thin one.

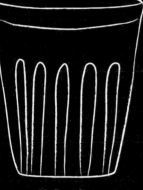

Medium glass
Perfect for a cold coffee, this is great for serving a small latte too. Beware as the glass can get quite hot.

Brandy snifter
The shape of the brandy snifter helps concentrate the aromas and entice your senses. Enjoy the aromas of a fruity Kenyan syphon in a brandy snifter.

Coupette
Serve iced coffee in a frosted coupette to add an elegant twist to a coffee cocktail. Decorate the rim for added presentation value.

Small bowl
Around the world, many communities traditionally drink coffee served in small bowls at social gatherings.

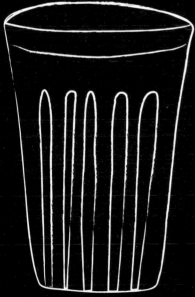

Large glass
When you want a cold drink on a hot day, a large glass will hold as much ice as you need to keep it cool.

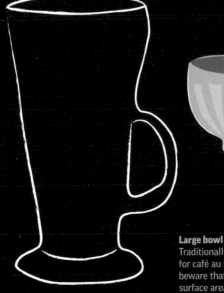

Latte glass
Synonymous with caffè lattes, this tall glass can showcase the pretty layers of any large coffee.

Large bowl
Traditionally used for café au lait, beware that a large surface area will cool your coffee quickly. Choose a thick, ceramic bowl to retain heat for as long as possible.

THE RECIPES

CAPPUCCINO

 GEAR **ESPRESSO**   DAIRY **MILK**   TEMP **HOT**   SERVES **2**

Most Italians drink their cappuccino in the mornings, but this classic breakfast coffee has now been adopted as an all-day drink worldwide. For many fans, the cappuccino represents the most harmonious ratio of coffee to milk.

WHAT DO I NEED?

Equipment
2 medium cups
espresso machine
milk pitcher

Ingredients
16–20g ($^1/_2$–$^3/_4$oz) fine
  ground coffee
about 130-150ml (4-5fl oz) milk
chocolate or cinnamon
  powder, optional

1 Warm your cups on top of your machine or by heating them with hot water. Using the technique on pp44–45, brew one shot/ 25ml (1fl oz) of espresso into each cup.

2 Steam the milk to about 60-65°C (140-150°F). Avoid scalding it. When the bottom of the pitcher is just too hot to touch, the milk is at a comfortable drinking temperature (see pp48–51).

TIP
This recipe shows you how to make two cups, but it is easy enough to make one – you can use a single basket and/or single spout portafilter. If all else fails, you could always treat a friend to the spare espresso!

HAVING OUTGROWN ITS ORIGINS AS AN **ITALIAN BREAKFAST DRINK,** THE **CAPPUCCINO** IS NOW **POPULAR** ALL OVER THE **WORLD**

3 Pour the milk over each espresso, maintaining an area of crema around the rim of the cup so that the first sip will have a strong coffee flavour. Aim for a 1cm (½in) layer of foam.

4 Using a shaker or a mini sieve, sprinkle over some chocolate or cinnamon powder, if desired.

CAFFÈ LATTE

 GEAR **ESPRESSO** DAIRY **MILK** TEMP **HOT** SERVES **1**

The caffè latte is another classic Italian breakfast beverage. It is milder in taste and heavier on the milk than all the other espresso-based recipes. It is now popular all over the world and is enjoyed throughout the day.

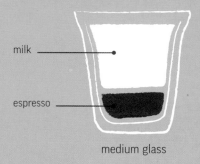

milk

espresso

medium glass

1 Warm the glass on top of your machine or by heating it with hot water. Using the technique on pp44–45, brew **one shot/25ml (1fl oz) of espresso** into your glass. If your glass does not fit under the spouts, brew your shots into a small jug instead.

2 Steam **about 210 ml (7fl oz) milk** (see pp48–51) to about 60–65°C (140–150°F), or until the pitcher is just too hot to touch.

3 If your espresso has been poured into a small jug, pour it into the glass. Pour the milk over the coffee, holding the jug close to the cup and pouring with a gentle side-to-side rocking motion. If desired, create a tulip latte art design, as shown on p54. Aim for a 5mm (¼in) layer of foam.

SERVE IT UP Serve immediately, with a spoon to stir. If you prefer a latte to have a crisp white layer of foam on top, simply brew your espresso into a small jug, then pour your milk into the glass first, followed by the espresso.

CHOOSE A COFFEE THAT HAS RICH COCOA OR NUTTY TONES TO COMPLEMENT THE SWEETNESS OF STEAMED MILK

FLAT WHITE

GEAR **ESPRESSO**   DAIRY **MILK**   TEMP **HOT**   SERVES **1**

Originally from Australia and New Zealand, this recipe varies from region to region. The flat white is similar to a cappuccino, but has a stronger coffee flavour, less foam, and is usually served with elaborate latte art on top.

milk

espresso

medium cup

1 Warm the cup on top of your machine or by heating it with hot water. Using the technique on pp44–45, brew **two shots/50ml (1½fl oz) of espresso** into the cup.

2 Steam **about 130ml (4fl oz) milk** (see pp48–51) to about 60–65°C (140–150°F), or until the pitcher is just too hot to touch.

3 Pour the milk over the coffee, holding the jug close to the cup and pouring with a gentle side-to-side rocking motion, using the techniques on pp52–55. Aim for a 5mm (¼in) layer of foam.

SERVE IT UP Serve immediately – the longer the drink is sat waiting, the more likely it is that the milk will lose its glossy shine.

TRY FRUITY OR NATURALLY PROCESSED COFFEES. COMBINED WITH MILK THEY BRING OUT A FLAVOUR REMINISCENT OF STRAWBERRY MILKSHAKE

RECOMMENDED COFFEE BEANS

BREVE

 GEAR **ESPRESSO**   DAIRY **MILK**   TEMP **HOT**   SERVES **2**

The breve is an American take on the classic latte. A twist on typical espresso-based beverages, it replaces half the milk with single cream (ideally with about 15 per cent fat content). Sweet and creamy, try it as an alternative to dessert.

WHAT DO I NEED?

Equipment
2 medium glasses or cups
espresso machine
milk pitcher

Ingredients
16–20g (¹/₂–³/₄oz) fine
  ground coffee
60ml (2fl oz) milk
60ml (2fl oz) single cream

TIP
Steaming with cream
is a different experience.
The sound while steaming
a combination of milk and
cream may be louder than
when you steam pure milk,
and will not result in
as much foam.

1 Warm the glasses or cups on top of your
machine or by heating them with hot water.
Using the technique on pp44–45, brew one
shot/25ml (1fl oz) of espresso into each glass.

BREVE TRANSLATES FROM **ITALIAN** INTO **"BRIEF" OR "SHORT"**. THE SINGLE CREAM HELPS TO CREATE A **FOAMY, DENSER DRINK**

2 Mix the milk and cream and steam to about 60–65°C (140–150°F), or until the pitcher is just too hot to touch (see pp48–51).

3 Pour the steamed milk and cream mixture over the espresso, allowing the crema and the thick foam to combine.

MACCHIATO

 GEAR **ESPRESSO**   DAIRY **MILK**   TEMP **HOT**   SERVES **2**

Another Italian classic, the macchiato gets its name from the custom of "marking" the espresso with milk foam, which lends a little more sweetness to the shot as you drink it. It is sometimes also called a caffè macchiato or an espresso macchiato.

WHAT DO I NEED?

Equipment
2 demitasse cups
espresso machine
milk pitcher

Ingredients
16–20g ($\frac{1}{2}$–$\frac{3}{4}$oz) fine
  ground coffee
100ml ($3\frac{1}{2}$fl oz) milk

1 Warm the cups on top of your machine or by heating them with hot water. Using the technique on pp44–45, brew one shot/25ml (1fl oz) of espresso into each cup.

YOU NEED ONLY THE SMALLEST
TOUCH OF MILK FOAM FOR AN
AUTHENTIC ITALIAN MACCHIATO.
IT ADDS A TOUCH OF SWEETNESS

TIP
While a traditional Italian
macchiato has only espresso
and milk foam, it is not unusual
to find versions elsewhere that
incorporate some of the warm
liquid milk that is created
when you steam to
make the foam.

2 Steam the milk (see pp48–51)
to about 60–65°C (140–150°F),
or until the pitcher is just too
hot to touch.

3 Carefully spoon 1–2 teaspoons of
foam on top of the crema of each
espresso shot, and serve.

CAFFÈ MOCHA

 GEAR **ESPRESSO**   DAIRY **MILK**   TEMP **HOT**   SERVES **2**

Coffee and dark chocolate are a classic flavour combination. Add chocolate pieces, shavings, or homemade or shop-bought chocolate sauce to a caffè latte or cappuccino to create a rich, slightly sweet, dessert-like beverage.

WHAT DO I NEED?

Equipment
2 large glasses
milk pitcher
espresso machine
small jug

Ingredients
4 tbsp dark chocolate sauce
   (see pp162–63)
400ml (14fl oz) milk
32–40g (1–1½oz) fine
   ground coffee

1 Measure out the chocolate sauce. Pour it into your glasses.

2 Steam the milk (see pp48–51) to about 60–65°C (140–150°F), or until the pitcher is just too hot to touch. Add enough air to create a foam layer of about 1cm (½in).

TIP
If you don't have chocolate sauce in hand, use some pieces of dark cooking chocolate or a few tablespoons of powdered hot chocolate mix. Mix them with a drop of milk first so they blend into the drink and don't go lumpy.

3 Pour the steamed milk carefully over the chocolate sauce in each glass to achieve a striking layered effect.

DARK CHOCOLATE IS MOST COMMONLY USED; TRY MILK CHOCOLATE OR A MIX OF THE TWO FOR A SWEETER FLAVOUR

4 Using the technique on pp44–45, brew two double shots/50ml (1^1/$_2$fl oz) of espresso into small jugs and pour them through the milk foam.

5 Serve as the espresso blends into the steamed milk. Stir gently with a long spoon to continue to dissolve and mix the ingredients.

TIP

For a uniform chocolate flavour, mix the milk with the chocolate sauce in the pitcher, and steam them together. Afterwards, make sure you thoroughly clean your steam wand inside out before you use it again.

CAFÉ AU LAIT

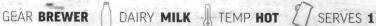 GEAR **BREWER** | DAIRY **MILK** | TEMP **HOT** | SERVES **1**

The classic French breakfast coffee with milk is traditionally served in a bowl with no handles, big enough to accommodate the dipping of a baguette. Picking up the bowl to drink will warm your hands on chilly mornings.

WHAT DO I NEED?

Equipment
drip or filter-style brewer
small saucepan
large bowl

Ingredients
180ml (6fl oz) strong filter coffee
180ml (6fl oz) milk

1 Prepare the coffee in your choice of drip or filter-style brewer (see pp128–37).

CHOOSING YOUR COFFEE

For an authentic flavour, choose a darker roast. The French have a tradition of roasting their coffee until it is a bit oily and bittersweet. This style works best of all when combined with a lot of sweet milk.

TIP

While the French press (see p128) might seem the most appropriate brewer for a café au lait, a lot of people in France use the stove-top moka pot at home (see p133), which can create a stronger brew.

SWEET MILK, WARMED SLOWLY ON THE STOVE, COMPLEMENTS A STRONG, DARK ROASTED FILTER COFFEE

TIP
If you want something to dip into your café au lait – but don't fancy the traditional French baguette – why not keep with the theme and choose a delicious flaky croissant or pain au chocolat?

2 Pour the milk into the small saucepan and set over a medium heat. Allow it to heat up gently for about 3–4 minutes, until 60–65°C (140–150°F).

3 Pour the brewed coffee into the bowl. Pour over the warm milk to taste, and enjoy.

ESPRESSO CON PANNA

GEAR **ESPRESSO**   DAIRY **CREAM**   TEMP **HOT**   SERVES **1**

Con panna is Italian for "with cream". A topping of luscious whipped cream can be added to any beverage – be it a cappuccino, caffè latte, or caffè mocha. It makes for a great presentation and adds a velvety quality to the drink.

 WHAT DO I NEED?

Equipment
demitasse cup or glass
espresso machine
whisk

Ingredients
16–20g (1/2–3/4oz) fine
   ground coffee
single cream, sweetened to taste

1 Warm the cup or glass on top of your machine or by heating it with hot water. Using the technique on pp44–45, brew a double shot/ 50ml (1 1/2fl oz) of espresso into the glass.

ADDING CREAM IS NOT SOLELY
AN ITALIAN PRACTICE. IN VIENNA,
A CAPPUCCINO IS OFTEN SERVED
WITH A LID OF WHIPPED CREAM

2 Pour the cream into a small bowl. Using a whisk, whip up the cream for a few minutes until it is stiff enough to hold its shape.

3 Spoon 1 tablespoon of whipped cream on top of the double espresso shot. Serve with a spoon for stirring.

TIP
If you prefer a softer taste, you can whisk the cream until thick but not stiff, and float it on top of the crema. This allows the espresso and cream to combine as you sip your coffee, diluting the double shot.

RISTRETTO AND LUNGO

GEAR **ESPRESSO** DAIRY **WITHOUT** TEMP **HOT** SERVES **2**

Alternatives to the "normale" espresso are "ristretto" and "lungo". All that changes is how much water you allow to pass through the grounds – you either restrict the extraction, or let the shots run long to wash out more solubles.

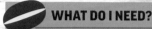

WHAT DO I NEED?

Equipment
espresso machine
2 demitasse glasses or cups

Ingredients
16–20g (½–¾oz) fine
 ground coffee per shot

RISTRETTO

The ristretto is espresso for the advanced drinker – an essence of coffee that leaves a strong, lingering aftertaste.

2 Stop the flow of water at about 15–20ml (1 tbsp–½fl oz) in each glass or cup (after 15–20 seconds), for a concentrated sip of coffee with a thick texture and intensified flavours.

1 Using the technique on pp44–45, brew one shot/25ml (1fl oz) of espresso into each glass or cup.

TIP
As an option, you can use a slightly finer grind or more coffee to restrict the water and extract more solubles, although these methods often result in increased bitterness, which you want to avoid.

RISTRETTO MEANS "RESTRICTED" AND LUNGO TRANSLATES AS "LONG". SURPRISINGLY, A RISTRETTO CONTAINS LESS CAFFEINE THAN A LUNGO

LUNGO

A softer version of the espresso, a lungo is brewed with an increased volume of water.

1 Using the technique on pp44–45, brew one shot/25ml (1fl oz) of espresso into each glass or cup.

2 Instead of turning off the flow of water into each glass or cup at around 25ml (1fl oz), or after 25–30 seconds, let it continue to brew through until you reach anything from 50–90ml (1½–3fl oz). Allowing an increased volume of water to pass through an amount of grounds intended for a normale espresso will result in a milder cup, thinner body, and higher astringency.

TIP
By brewing a lungo into a 90ml (3fl oz) demitasse glass or cup, you have an easy measure of volume that helps you to know when to cut the flow of water, and avoids any excessive compromise of flavour.

AMERICANO

 GEAR **ESPRESSO**   DAIRY **WITHOUT**   TEMP **HOT**   SERVES **1**

During World War II, American soldiers in Europe found the local espresso too strong. They diluted the shots with hot water creating the Americano – a brew similar in strength to filter coffee, with some of the flavours of an espresso.

 WHAT DO I NEED?

Equipment
medium cup
espresso machine

Ingredients
16–20g ($^1/_2$–$^3/_4$oz) fine
ground coffee

TIP
An alternative method is to fill the cup with hot water first, leaving room for two shots/ 50ml (1½fl oz) of espresso. This helps to keep the crema floating on the surface – which some prefer for presentation.

1 Warm the cup on top of your machine or by heating it with hot water. Using the technique on pp44–45, brew two shots/ 50ml (1½fl oz) of espresso into the cup.

AMERICANOS RETAIN THE TEXTURE FROM THE OILS AND SOLUBLES OF THE ESPRESSO, BUT SOFTEN THE BREW INTENSITY

TIP

If you're not sure how strong to make it, serve the water in a jug on the side and fill the cup half-three-quarters full, tasting and adding more if desired. This is a great way to make a long cup of coffee using your espresso machine.

2 Carefully pour in boiling water, as desired, over the double espresso. There is no correct ratio, but try one part espresso to four parts water to start with, and add more if you prefer.

3 If you prefer, you could remove the crema with a spoon – some like this because it results in a cleaner, less bitter flavoured coffee. You can remove the crema before or after adding the water – both are valid methods.

SYRUPS AND FLAVOURINGS

Great coffee has clear and complex flavours that purists would not blend or dilute with other ingredients. However, homemade or shop-bought syrups and sauces often appeal to those who enjoy coffee as a dessert-like treat.

SIMPLE SYRUP

This clear sweetening agent is typically made with white sugar, but you can also try brown for a caramelized taste and colour. To flavour, add approximately 30ml (1fl oz) of a fruit, herb, or nut extract, such as almond, banana, mint, or cherry.

Makes 500ml (16fl oz)

Method

1 In a large saucepan, bring **500ml (16fl oz) water** to the boil over a medium heat.

2 Stir in **500g (1lb 2oz) white sugar** until it dissolves. Remove from the heat.

3 Cool and transfer to a sterilized, airtight jar or bottle, and store in the fridge. It will keep for approximately two weeks. Add **1 tablespoon vodka**, if desired, to double its shelf-life.

CARAMEL SAUCE

A homemade caramel sauce makes a rich alternative to sugar or simple syrup when you want some extra sweetness.

Makes 200ml (7fl oz)

Method

1 Heat **200g (7oz) sugar** and **60ml (2fl oz) water** in a heavy-based pan over a medium heat, stirring continuously.

2 Once it starts to bubble, stop stirring and simmer until it reaches 115°C (240°F). Remove from the heat and stir in **3 tablespoons unsalted butter** and **½ teaspoon sea salt**.

3 Carefully add **120ml (4fl oz) heavy cream** while whisking. Stir until it is smooth, then add **1 teaspoon vanilla extract** and mix.

4 Cool and transfer to a sterilized, airtight jar or bottle, and store in the fridge. It will keep for approximately two to three weeks.

FLAVOURING

CHAI POWDER
Combine 1 tablespoon each or equal parts of ground cardamom, allspice, cinnamon, cloves, ginger, black pepper, nutmeg, and liquorice root. Store in an airtight box and use to flavour tea-coffee blends (see Chai coffee p184).

STRAWBERRY SYRUP

Strawberry is a flavour often found in coffees, especially when they have been naturally processed. Enhance the flavour and add a natural and sweet berry note with a dash of homemade strawberry syrup.

Makes 600ml (1 pint)

Method

1 Place **500g (1lb 2oz) roughly chopped strawberries** in a saucepan and pour over **500ml (16fl oz) water.**

2 Bring to the boil and simmer for 25 minutes. Skim off any foam that gathers on the surface.

3 Remove from the heat and strain out the liquid without squeezing the strawberries.

4 Add **225g (8oz) sugar** to the liquid and bring to the boil while stirring. Simmer until the sugar dissolves, and skim off any foam that gathers on the surface.

5 Cool and transfer to a sterilized, airtight jar or bottle, and store in the fridge. It will keep for approximately two weeks.

FLAVOURING

GINGERBREAD BUTTER
Mix 2 tablespoons of soft, lightly salted butter with 100g (3½oz) brown sugar, ¼ teaspoon each of ground allspice, nutmeg, cinnamon, cloves, and 2 teaspoons of rum essence in a bowl. Use as a topping on coffees (see p182).

CHOCOLATE SAUCE

Whether you are making a mocha or a hot chocolate, a homemade chocolate sauce is best. A dash of salt will counteract the bitterness of the cocoa powder and make the chocolate flavour more pronounced.

Makes 250ml (9fl oz)

Method

1 In a medium saucepan, mix **125g (4½oz) cocoa powder, 150g (5½oz) sugar**, and **pinch of salt**, if desired, together.

2 Add **250ml (9fl oz) water** and bring to the boil over a medium heat, whisking continuously. Allow to simmer for 5 minutes while stirring.

3 Remove from the heat and mix in **1 teaspoon vanilla flavouring**.

4 Cool and transfer to a sterilized, airtight jar or bottle, and store in the fridge. It will keep for about two to three weeks.

ROMANO

 GEAR **ESPRESSO**   DAIRY **WITHOUT**   TEMP **HOT**   SERVES **1**

It is easy to put a spin on the flavour of espresso without adding lots
of ingredients. A simple lemon twist lends a fresh, citrussy undertone
to the espresso – making this a potent classic.

espresso

demitasse cup

1 Using the technique on pp44–45, brew **two shots/50ml (1½fl oz)
of espresso** into the cup.

2 Using **1 lemon**, make a twist of peel using a channel knife
or zester.

3 Rub the peel gently around the rim of the cup, and let it hang
over the edge.

SERVE IT UP Sweeten to taste with **demerara sugar**, and
serve immediately.

RED EYE

 GEAR **BREWER AND ESPRESSO**   DAIRY **WITHOUT**   TEMP **HOT**   SERVES **1**

If you can't quite get started in the mornings or need a caffeine-fuelled kick
to keep you going through the day, try the Red Eye, also lovingly nicknamed
The Alarm Clock in gratitude of its invigorating caffeine content.

espresso

brewed coffee

large mug

1 Brew **12g (¼oz) medium-ground coffee** using a French press (see p128),
AeroPress (see p131), or brewer of your choice. Pour 200ml (7fl oz)
brewed coffee into the mug.

2 Using the technique on pp44–45, brew **two shots/50ml (1½fl oz)
of espresso** into a small jug.

SERVE IT UP Pour the espresso into the brewed coffee and
serve immediately.

CUBANO

GEAR **ESPRESSO**   DAIRY **WITHOUT**   TEMP **HOT**   SERVES **1**

Also called Cuban shot or Cafecito, this short and sweet coffee is a popular drink in Cuba. When brewed through the espresso machine, the sugar creates a smooth, sweet espresso shot. Use it as a base for numerous coffee cocktails.

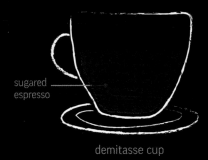

sugared espresso

demitasse cup

1 Mix **14–18g (½–¾oz) ground espresso coffee** with **2 teaspoons demerara sugar**, and place the mix in the portafilter of your espresso machine (see p44, steps 1–3).

2 Brew the coffee and sugar through the machine, until your cup is about half full.

SERVE IT UP Serve immediately. If desired, use as base for alcoholic espresso-based cocktails (see pp205–17).

SASSY MOLASSES

GEAR **ESPRESSO**   DAIRY **WITHOUT**   TEMP **HOT**   SERVES **1**

Sassafras is a flowering, fruit-bearing tree native to eastern North America and eastern Asia. The extract from its bark is typically used to flavour root beers. Choose a safrole-free version of sassafras for any recipe you work with.

molasses espresso with sassafras

demitasse cup

1 Spoon **1 teaspoon molasses** into your demitasse cup.

2 Using the technique on pp44–45, brew **two shots/50ml (1½fl oz) of espresso** over the molasses.

SERVE IT UP Add **5 drops sassafras root extract**, and serve immediately with a stirring spoon.

CAFFÈ TOUBA This spiced drink is gaining popularity in other cities — both in and outside of Senegal.

CAFFÈ TOUBA *Senegalese coffee*

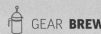 GEAR **BREWER**   DAIRY **WITHOUT**   TEMP **HOT**   SERVES **4**

Caffè Touba is a spicy drink from Senegal, named after the holy city of Touba. Green coffee beans are roasted with peppers and spices, crushed in a mortar and pestle, and brewed through a cloth filter. It can be sweetened to taste.

filtered
spiced
coffee

large mug

1 Roast **60g (2oz) green coffee beans** with **1 teaspoon selim pepper grains** and **1 teaspoon cloves** in a wok over a medium heat. Stir continuously.

2 Once you have reached the desired roast (see pp66–67), remove the beans from the wok and allow to cool. Stir.

3 Crush the coffee beans and spices finely in a mortar and pestle. Place the coffee in a cloth filter (see p130) and mount it on a serving jug. Pour **500ml (16fl oz) boiling water**.

SERVE IT UP Sweeten with **sugar**, divide between the mugs, and serve.

SCANDINAVIAN COFFEE

 GEAR **BREWER**   DAIRY **WITHOUT**   TEMP **WARM**   SERVES **4**

The practice of adding egg to the brewing process might seem unusual, but the proteins in the egg bind the sour and bitter components of coffee together. This results in a mild drink with all the body of a non-paper filtered brew.

coffee–egg
brew

large mug

1 Mix **60g (2oz) coarse-ground coffee**, **1 egg**, and **60ml (2 fl oz) cold water** together to make a paste.

2 Pour **1 litre (1¾ pints) water** into a saucepan and bring to the boil. Add the paste, stirring gently.

3 Allow to boil for 3 minutes. Remove from the heat, add **100ml (3½fl oz) cold water**, and let the grounds settle.

SERVE IT UP Divide the coffee between the mugs, pouring it through a fine mesh or cheesecloth to filter, and serve.

BUNA *Ethiopian coffee ceremony*

GEAR **BREWER**   DAIRY **WITHOUT**   TEMP **HOT**   SERVES **10**

Ethiopians drink buna during ceremonies with family and friends. Frankincense burns on the coals while coffee is roasted and served from a traditional "jebena". The grounds are brewed three times, resulting in three very different cups of coffee.

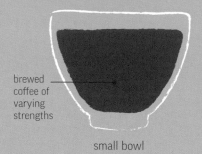

brewed coffee of varying strengths

small bowl

1 Roast **100g (3½oz) green coffee beans** in a pan over a medium heat. Stir until they are dark and oily. In a mortar and pestle, crush them fine.

2 Pour **1 litre (1¾ pints) water** into a jebena or saucepan over a medium heat, and bring to the boil. Add the ground coffee and stir. Steep for 5 minutes.

SERVE IT UP Pour out 10 bowls of the first brew, avoiding the grounds. Serve. Add another **1 litre (1¾ pints) water** to the pan, allow to boil, then divide among the bowls for the second brew. Finally, add another **1 litre (1¾ pints) water**, repeat the process, and serve the weakest brew.

I'M YOUR HUCKLEBERRY

GEAR **BREWER**   DAIRY **WITHOUT**   TEMP **HOT**   SERVES **1**

Huckleberries, the state fruits of Idaho, look and taste like blueberries. A lot of apples grow in Idaho, and apple flavours often feature in the high-quality coffee served there. This tribute to the region incorporates apple in the steeping time.

apple flavouring

huckleberry flavouring

brewed coffee

large mug

1 Brew **250ml (9fl oz) coffee** and **a few apple slices** in a filter pour-over (see p129) or other brewer. If you use a pour-over, place the apple on the coffee grounds and pour water over the top. With a French press (see p128), add the apple and coffee into the pot then pour over the water.

2 Pour the coffee into your mug, and add **25ml (1fl oz) huckleberry flavouring** and **1 tablespoon apple flavouring**.

SERVE IT UP Garnish with a **lime twist** and some **apple slices**. Sweeten with **simple syrup** (see pp162–63) and serve.

CAFFÈ DE OLLA *Mexican brew*

 GEAR **BREWER**   DAIRY **WITHOUT**   TEMP **HOT**   SERVES **1**

An olla – the traditional clay pot used to brew this Mexican drink – lends an earthy dimension to the brew. If you don't have an olla, a regular saucepan still allows the texture and oil from the beans to give the brew extra body.

sweetened cinnamon coffee

earthenware mug

1 In a saucepan over a medium heat, bring **500ml (16fl oz) water**, **2 cinnamon sticks**, and **50g (1³⁄₄oz) piloncillo or dark brown sugar** to the boil and simmer, stirring constantly until the sugar is dissolved.

2 Remove the pan from the heat, cover, and steep for 5 minutes. Add **30g (1oz) medium-ground coffee** and steep for another 5 minutes. Strain the mixture through a fine-wire mesh or cheesecloth into the mug.

SERVE IT UP Serve with a cinnamon stick – it looks good and imparts a more pronounced flavour.

TURKISH COFFEE

 GEAR **BREWER**   DAIRY **WITHOUT**   TEMP **HOT**   SERVES **4**

You prepare Turkish coffee in an ibrik, cezve, or briki (see p137), which are small coffee pots with one long handle. Served in small bowls, the finished brew has a layer of foam on top and heavy sediment at the bottom.

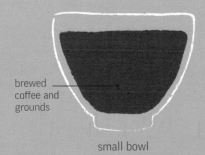

brewed coffee and grounds

small bowl

1 Add **120ml (4fl oz) water** and **2 tablespoons sugar** into a Turkish coffee pot or saucepan and bring to the boil over a medium heat.

2 Remove from the heat and add **4 tablespoons superfine-grind coffee**. Add **cardamom**, **cinnamon**, or **nutmeg**, **if desired**, stirring to dissolve.

3 Brew the coffee as shown on p137. Spoon some of the foam into 4 bowls and carefully pour the coffee in so the foam does not dissipate.

SERVE IT UP Allow to settle for a couple of minutes, and serve. Take care to stop sipping when you reach the grounds at the bottom of the bowl.

MADHA ALAY coffee is inspired by the Marathi people of Maharashtra, western India.

MADHA ALAY

🫖 GEAR **BREWER**   🍼 DAIRY **WITHOUT**   🌡 TEMP **HOT**   🥤 SERVES **2**

A concoction of ginger, honey, and lemon is the perfect remedy if you feel a cold coming on, and works very well with a splash of whisky. Using coffee prepared in a stove-top pot (see p133), it makes enough for two small glasses.

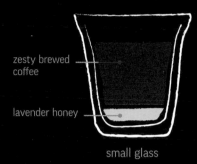

zesty brewed coffee

lavender honey

small glass

1 Using the technique on p133, brew **32g (1oz) coarse-ground coffee** in a 300ml (10fl oz) stove-top pot.

2 Spoon **1 tablespoon lavender honey** into each glass, **1cm (½in) piece chopped fresh root ginger** and **peel from ½ lemon** between the glasses.

3 Boil **250ml (9fl oz) water**. Pour over the mixture, filling half of each glass. Allow to steep for a minute.

SERVE IT UP Pour over 75ml (2½fl oz) freshly brewed coffee into each glass. Stir to help dissolve the honey, and serve with a spoon.

KOPI JAHE *Indonesian coffee*

🫖 GEAR **BREWER**   🍼 DAIRY **WITHOUT**   🌡 TEMP **HOT**   🥤 SERVES **6**

In Indonesia, the boiling of fresh ginger and sugar with ground coffee makes Kopi Jahe, an aromatic brew. The name means "coffee ginger" in Bahasa. Add spices such as cinnamon or cloves to the process for added flavour.

sweet ginger coffee

large cups

1 Bring **6 tablespoons medium-ground coffee**, **1.5 litres (2¾ pints) water**, **7.5cm (3in) piece crushed fresh root ginger**, **100g (3½oz) palm sugar**, and, if desired, **2 cinnamon sticks and/or 3 cloves** to the boil in a saucepan over a medium heat. Reduce to a simmer, stirring until the sugar dissolves.

2 Remove from the heat when you have extracted the ginger to taste, about 5 minutes.

SERVE IT UP Divide between the six cups, straining through a cheesecloth, and serve immediately.

VANILLA WARMER

🍼 GEAR **BREWER**   🥛 DAIRY **WITHOUT**   🌡 TEMP **HOT**   🥤 SERVES **2**

When exploring flavours that complement coffee, very little beats the pure simplicity of vanilla. There are many forms of vanilla to play with, such as whole pods (used here), powdered, syrup, essence, and even alcoholic spirits.

brewed vanilla coffee

large mug

1 Split open **2 vanilla pods**. Add the seeds to a saucepan filled with **500ml (16fl oz) water** over a medium heat. Allow to boil, then remove from the heat, set the pods aside, and add **30g (1oz) coarse-ground coffee** to the pan. Cover with a lid and allow to sit for 5 minutes.

2 Meanwhile, using a pastry brush, brush the insides of two mugs with **1 tablespoon vanilla flavouring**.

SERVE IT UP Strain the coffee through a cheesecloth into the mugs, add the pods, and serve.

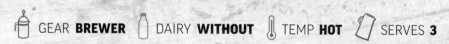

SYPHON SPICE

🍼 GEAR **BREWER**   🥛 DAIRY **WITHOUT**   🌡 TEMP **HOT**   🥤 SERVES **3**

Syphon brewers (see p132) are perfect for infusing coffee grounds with spices, whether whole or ground. If you do add flavourings, it's best to use a paper or metal syphon filter, keeping the cloth filters purely for coffee preparation.

brewed spiced coffee

medium cup

1 Place **2 whole cloves** and **3 whole allspice** in the lower bulb of a regular 3-cup, or 360ml (12fl oz), syphon. Fill with **300ml (10fl oz) water**.

2 Mix **¼ teaspoon ground nutmeg** with **15g (½oz) medium-ground coffee** and add to the water once it has travelled to the upper glass. Allow the coffee and nutmeg to infuse for a minute before removing the flame. Watch as the coffee drains back down.

SERVE IT UP Pour into three cups, and serve.

CALCUTTA COFFEE

GEAR **BREWER**   DAIRY **WITHOUT**   TEMP **HOT**   SERVES **4**

In many parts of the world, coffee is substituted with ground chicory, the roasted and ground root of the herbaceous plant. Give this beverage an exotic spin by adding some ground mace and a few saffron threads.

brewed
spiced
coffee

medium mug

1 Pour **1 litre (1¾ pints) water** into a saucepan. Add **1 teaspoon ground mace** and **a few saffron threads**, and bring to the boil over a medium heat.

2 Remove from the heat and add **40g (1½ oz) medium-ground coffee** and **20g (¾ oz) medium-ground chicory**. Cover and steep for 5 minutes.

SERVE IT UP Strain through a paper filter into a jug. Divide between the mugs, and serve.

KAISER MELANGE *Austrian coffee*

GEAR **ESPRESSO**   DAIRY **WHIPPED CREAM**   TEMP **HOT**   SERVES **1**

This Austrian recipe uses egg yolk and coffee, a combination also popular in Scandinavia. Combined with honey the egg yolk gives this espresso a voluptuous texture, and the optional brandy will add another layer of flavour.

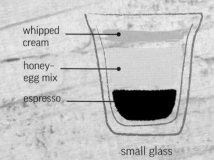

whipped
cream

honey–
egg mix

espresso

small glass

1 Using the technique on pp44–45, brew **one shot/25ml (1fl oz) of espresso** into your glass. Add **25ml (1fl oz) brandy, if desired**.

2 In a small bowl, combine **1 egg yolk** with **1 teaspoon honey**. Gently pour it over the espresso so it floats on the surface.

SERVE IT UP Top with **1 tablespoon whipped cream** and serve immediately.

COCONUT–EGG COFFEE

GEAR **BREWER** DAIRY **WITHOUT** TEMP **HOT** SERVES **1**

Inspired by Vietnamese egg coffee, this recipe replaces condensed milk with cream of coconut, lending another dimension to the taste and making the recipe suitable for those with a dairy intolerance.

coconut–egg mix

brewed coffee

medium glass

1 Brew **120ml (4fl oz) coffee** using a phin (see p136). Alternatively, brew it in a French press (see p128). Pour into your glass.

2 Whisk **1 egg yolk** and **2 teaspoons cream of coconut** together until fluffy. Gently spoon the mixture over the coffee, so it floats.

SERVE IT UP Sweeten to taste with **demerara sugar**, and serve with a spoon.

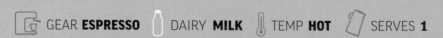

HONEY BLOSSOM

GEAR **ESPRESSO** DAIRY **MILK** TEMP **HOT** SERVES **1**

As honey bees feed on various flowers and herbs, the honey they produce takes on some of the properties from the nectar. Orange blossoms are one such source, and a water distillate highlights their flavour in this recipe.

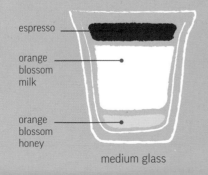

espresso

orange blossom milk

orange blossom honey

medium glass

1 Steam **150ml (5fl oz) milk** in a pitcher with **1 tablespoon orange blossom water** to about 60–65°C (140–150°F), or until the pitcher is just too hot to touch (see pp48–50). Aim for about a 1cm (½in) layer of foam.

2 Spoon **1 tablespoon orange blossom honey** into the bottom of the glass and pour the milk over.

3 Using the technique on pp44–45, brew **one shot/25ml (1fl oz) of espresso** into a jug. Pour the espresso into the glass, through the foam.

SERVE IT UP Serve with a spoon for stirring, to help dissolve the honey.

EGGNOG LATTE

GEAR **ESPRESSO**   DAIRY **MILK**   TEMP **HOT**   SERVES **1**

This latte is moreish and rich, making the most of a holiday favourite. Shop-bought eggnog does not usually contain raw egg, but if you choose to make your own, beware of the risks of contamination and curdling when hot.

espresso

eggnog milk

medium cup or glass

1 Gently heat **150ml (5fl oz) eggnog** and **75ml (2½fl oz) milk** in a saucepan over a medium heat, stirring continuously. Do not allow to boil. Pour the warm eggnog mixture into the cup or glass.

2 Using the technique on pp44–45, brew **two shots/50ml (1½fl oz) of espresso** into a small jug, and pour it over the eggnog mixture.

SERVE IT UP Grate some **fresh nutmeg** over the top, and serve.

SOYA EGGNOG LATTE

GEAR **ESPRESSO**   DAIRY **SOYA MILK**   TEMP **HOT**   SERVES **1**

Choose a good-quality brand of soya milk and soya eggnog for this dairy-free alternative to the classic eggnog latte. You can add brandy or bourbon to make it a grownup drink, or replace nutmeg with chocolate shavings.

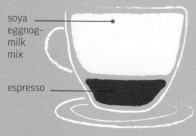

soya eggnog-milk mix

espresso

large cup

1 Heat **100ml (3½fl oz) soya eggnog** and **100ml (3½fl oz) soya milk** in a saucepan over a medium heat. Do not allow to boil.

2 Using the technique on pp44–45, brew **two shots/50ml (1½fl oz) of espresso** into the cup.

3 Add the warm eggnog–milk mixture into the cup over the espresso, and stir.

SERVE IT UP Add **a dash of brandy, if desired**, sprinkle with **ground nutmeg**, and serve.

MAPLE PECAN

GEAR **ESPRESSO**   DAIRY **MILK**   TEMP **HOT**   SERVES **1**

Combining espresso with good-quality maple syrup and pecans makes this taste like liquid pecan pie. Serve some shortbread on the side, and enjoy it dunked in your coffee.

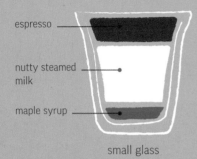

espresso

nutty steamed milk

maple syrup

small glass

1 Steam **120ml (4fl oz) milk** in a pitcher with **5 drops pecan flavouring** to about 60–65°C (140–150°F), or until the pitcher is just too hot to touch (see pp48–51). Aim for about a 1.5cm (½in) layer of nutty, sweet foam.

2 Pour **1 tablespoon maple syrup** into the bottom of the glass and pour the milk over the top.

3 Using the technique on pp44–45, brew **two shots/50ml (1½fl oz) of espresso** into a jug, and pour into the glass.

SERVE IT UP Decorate with **1 pecan nut**, and serve with a spoon to stir through the maple syrup.

CHERRY ALMOND LATTE

GEAR **ESPRESSO**   DAIRY **ALMOND MILK**   TEMP **HOT**   SERVES **1**

For a flavoured caffè latte that is also dairy free, try steaming almond milk, an alternative that suits those with a dairy intolerance. Here, the almond milk lends a nutty flavour and is complemented by the sweet cherry extract.

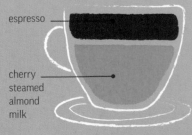

espresso

cherry steamed almond milk

large cup

1 Steam **150ml (5fl oz) almond milk** with **25ml (1fl oz) cherry flavouring** to about 60–65°C (140–150°F), or until the pitcher is just too hot to touch (see pp48–51). Pour into the cup.

2 Using the technique on pp44–45, brew **two shots/50ml (1½fl oz) of espresso** into a small jug and pour over the top of the milk.

SERVE IT UP Serve with a stirring spoon.

ALMOND FIG LATTE

GEAR **BREWER** · DAIRY **MILK** · TEMP **HOT** · SERVES **1**

Figs are used as a flavour enhancer in many coffees around the world, but rarely as an ingredient in a beverage. It is combined here with almond essence, which gives this variation of a caffè latte real depth of flavour.

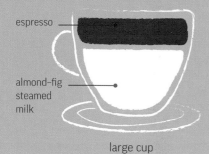

espresso

almond–fig steamed milk

large cup

1 Steam **250ml (9fl oz) milk** with **1 teaspoon almond essence** and **5 drops fig flavouring** in a pitcher to about 60–65°C (140–150°F), or until the pitcher is just too hot to touch (see pp48–51). Pour into the cup.

2 Brew **100ml (3½fl oz) coffee** using a French press (see p128), AeroPress (see p131), or brewer of your choice. Brew the coffee double-strength, if you prefer a more pronounced coffee taste.

SERVE IT UP Pour the brewed coffee over the flavoured steamed milk, and serve.

MOCHI AFFOGATO

GEAR **ESPRESSO** · DAIRY **COCONUT MILK ICE CREAM** · TEMP **HOT** · SERVES **1**

A popular Japanese dessert, Mochi ice cream is a ball of cold ice cream covered in a smooth, dough-like rice paste. This recipe uses a Mochi made with coconut milk, making it suitable for those with a dairy intolerance.

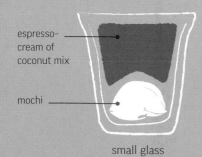

espresso– cream of coconut mix

mochi

small glass

1 Place **1 black sesame-flavoured coconut milk mochi** in your glass.

2 Using the technique on pp44–45, brew **two shots/50ml (1½fl oz) of espresso** into a small jug.

3 Mix **50ml (1½fl oz) cream of coconut** with the espresso and pour it over the mochi.

SERVE IT UP Serve immediately with a spoon.

AFFOGATO

GEAR **ESPRESSO**   DAIRY **ICE CREAM**   TEMP **HOT AND COLD**   SERVES **1**

This is one of the simplest of all espresso-based treats. A scoop of ice cream drowned in strong espresso makes for a perfect end to any meal. Choose egg-free vanilla ice cream for a light version, or add flavoured ice cream for variety.

espresso

vanilla ice cream

small glass

1 Spoon **1 scoop of vanilla ice cream** into your glass. It looks most attractive if you can form a full ball of ice cream using a scoop.

2 Using the technique on pp44–45, brew **two shots/50ml (1½fl oz) of espresso** and pour it over the ice cream.

SERVE IT UP Serve with a spoon to eat as a dessert, or allow to melt while sipping.

ALMOND AFFOGATO

GEAR **ESPRESSO**   DAIRY **ALMOND MILK**   TEMP **HOT AND COLD**   SERVES **1**

Almond milk is a great alternative if you are lactose-intolerant. Made of ground almonds and water and sweetened to taste, almond milk and ice cream are easy to make at home. Enjoy the fresh flavours they can bring to your coffee.

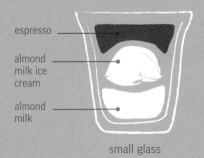

espresso

almond milk ice cream

almond milk

small glass

1 Pour **25ml (1fl oz) almond milk** into a small glass. Top with **1 scoop almond milk ice cream**.

2 Using the technique on pp44–45, brew **one shot/25ml (1fl oz) of espresso** into a small jug. Pour it over the ice cream.

SERVE IT UP Sprinkle over **½ teaspoon cinnamon** and **1 teaspoon chopped almonds**, and serve.

ALMOND AFFOGATO is a delicious dairy-free coffee recipe. If you are allergic, try rice milk with rice milk ice cream.

YUANYANG *Hong Kong coffee*

GEAR **BREWER**   DAIRY **CONDENSED MILK**   TEMP **HOT**   SERVES **4**

Most people would not think to mix tea and coffee together, but this creamy mix with black tea has delicious results. Originally served by street vendors, yuanyang is now a favourite in many Hong Kong restaurants.

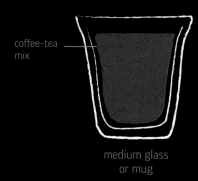

coffee-tea mix

medium glass or mug

1 Combine **2 tablespoons black tea leaves** and **250ml (9fl oz) water** in a large 1 litre (1¾ pints) saucepan, and simmer for 2 minutes.

2 Remove the saucepan from the heat, and discard the tea leaves. Stir in **250ml (9fl oz) condensed milk**, return to the heat, and simmer for another 2 minutes. Remove from the heat.

3 Using the technique on p128, brew **500ml (16fl oz) coffee** in a French press and pour into the saucepan. Mix thoroughly with a wooden spoon.

SERVE IT UP Pour into 4 glasses or mugs, sweeten with **sugar**, and serve.

STRAWBERRY LACE

GEAR **BREWER**   DAIRY **MILK**   TEMP **HOT**   SERVES **1**

Many of us enjoy strawberries dipped in melted dark chocolate, and many more enjoy strawberries and cream. Substituting dark chocolate for white in this recipe bridges the two desserts and adds a lovely creaminess.

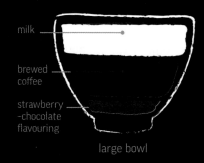

milk

brewed coffee

strawberry -chocolate flavouring

large bowl

1 Brew **150ml (5fl oz) coffee** in a French press (see p128), AeroPress (see p131), or brewer of your choice.

2 Heat **150ml (5fl oz) milk** in a saucepan over a medium heat, but do not allow to boil.

3 Pour **2 tablespoons white chocolate** and **1 tablespoon strawberry flavouring** (see pp162–63) into the bottom of the bowl. Add the coffee and milk.

SERVE IT UP Serve with a spoon, to stir and dissolve the chocolate.

BANANA SPILT

GEAR **BREWER**   DAIRY **MILK**   TEMP **HOT**   SERVES **1**

If you like classic banana-based desserts like banoffee pie or banana split, you'll enjoy this drink because it emulates some of their iconic flavours. Serve in a 300ml (10fl oz) welled coupette glass for a beautiful presentation.

milk
brewed coffee
caramel sauce
condensed milk

coupette glass

1 Pour **1 teaspoon condensed milk** into the well of the coupette glass. Add **1 teaspoon caramel sauce** over the top.

2 Add **5 drops banana flavouring** (see pp162–63) to the glass. Brew **100ml (3½fl oz) coffee** in a French press (see p128), AeroPress (see p131), or brewer of your choice.

3 Heat **100ml (3½fl oz) milk** in a pan over a medium heat, but don't allow to boil.

SERVE IT UP Pour the coffee and milk into the glass, and serve with a spoon.

CA PHE SUA NONG *Vietnamese coffee*

GEAR **BREWER**   DAIRY **CONDENSED MILK**   TEMP **HOT**   SERVES **1**

You don't have to use a Vietnamese phin coffee dripper to make Ca phe sua nong, but it's a clean and easy-to-use brewing method that also lends itself well to black coffee. Here, condensed milk makes for a sweet and creamy drink.

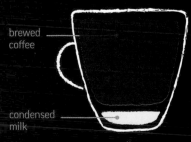

brewed coffee

condensed milk

small mug

1 Pour **2 tablespoons condensed milk** into the bottom of the mug. Place **2 tablespoons medium-ground coffee** at the bottom of a phin (see p136) or filter pour-over (see p129). Shake to distribute and screw the top filter on.

2 Bring **120ml (4fl oz) water** to the boil and pour about a third of it over the filter. Allow the coffee to swell for a minute. Loosen the filter a couple of turns and pour the rest of the water on. The water should drip through in about 5 minutes.

SERVE IT UP Serve with a spoon, to stir and dissolve the condensed milk.

POT OF GOLD

 GEAR **BREWER**   DAIRY **WITHOUT**   TEMP **HOT**    SERVES **1**

If you are lactose intolerant, there are plenty of lactose-free milks to explore, including nut and seed milks. This recipe includes raw egg, which adds a wonderful creaminess. The glowing gold custard that decorates the drink inspired the name.

non-dairy whipped cream

eggy custard

brewed coffee

small mug

1 Using the technique on p133, brew **100ml (3½fl oz) strong stove-top coffee**.

2 To make the eggy custard, separate **1 egg** and discard the white. Mix the yolk and **2 tablespoons lactose-free custard** in a small bowl. Add 1 teaspoon of the coffee and blend it in.

SERVE IT UP Pour the coffee into the mug and top with the eggy custard. Top up with **non-dairy whipped cream**, sprinkle over **vanilla sugar, if desired**, and serve.

GINGERBREAD GROG

 GEAR **BREWER**   DAIRY **SINGLE CREAM**   TEMP **HOT**   SERVES **6**

Beautifully fragrant and deliciously warming on a cold night, this drink may take a few minutes to prepare, but it will be worth the wait. Perfect after a good meal, the richness of the butter and sugar makes it a great alternative to dessert.

coffee–cream mix

large mug

1 Place an equal amount of sliced **peel from 1 lemon** and **1 orange** in the mugs.

2 Brew **1.5 litres (2¾ pints) coffee** using a French press (see p128) or electric-filter brew (see p135).

3 Pour into a jug and add **250ml (9fl oz) single cream**. Pour the coffee–cream mix over the citrus peels.

SERVE IT UP Divide the **gingerbread butter** (see pp162–63) between the mugs, about 1 teaspoon in each. Allow to melt, and serve.

GINGERBREAD GROG As the
flavoured butter melts and the spices
dissolve, little pearls form on the surface.

CHAI COFFEE

GEAR **BREWER**   DAIRY **MILK**   TEMP **HOT**   SERVES **1**

While you can buy ready-mixed Indian chai tea flavourings, making your own is easy (as shown on pp162–63). You can adjust the spice mix to suit your taste, and it keeps for up to 1 month in a sealed container.

milky
tea-coffee
blend

large mug

1 Add **1 teaspoon chai tea flavouring** (see pp162–63) to a small saucepan filled with **100ml (3½fl oz) water**. Add **1 teaspoon loose-leaf black tea** and bring the mix to the boil. Allow to simmer for 5 minutes.

2 Add **100ml (3½fl oz) milk** and allow it to heat up, but not boil. Meanwhile, brew **100ml (3½fl oz) coffee** using a French press (see p128), AeroPress (see p131), or brewer of your choice. Strain out the tea leaves and spice mixture.

SERVE IT UP Mix the milky tea with an equal amount of coffee in the mug, sweeten to taste with **sugar**, and serve.

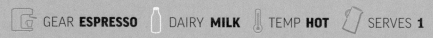

CHOC–MINT LIQUORICE

GEAR **ESPRESSO**   DAIRY **MILK**   TEMP **HOT**   SERVES **1**

The slightly savoury quality of liquorice, dark chocolate bitterness, and freshness of mint make this a grownup drink. Add less milk to ration it down to a more intensely flavoured drink.

espresso

mint-flavoured
milk

sweet liquorice
sauce

medium glass

1 Add **1–2 chocolate pieces** and **1 tablespoon sweet liquorice sauce** to the bottom of the glass.

2 Steam **150ml (5fl oz) milk** in a pitcher with **5–6 drops mint flavouring** to about 60–65°C (140–150°F), or until the pitcher is just too hot to touch (see pp48–51). Pour into the glass.

3 Using the technique on pp44–45, brew **two shots/50ml (1½fl oz) of espresso** into a small jug.

SERVE IT UP Pour the espresso through the milk foam, and serve.

MAZAGRAN *Portuguese iced coffee*

GEAR **ESPRESSO**   DAIRY **WITHOUT**   TEMP **COLD**   SERVES **1**

A Portuguese variation of cold coffee, Mazagran is made with strong coffee or espresso. It is served over ice with a twist of lemon, slightly sweetened, and occasionally spiked with rum.

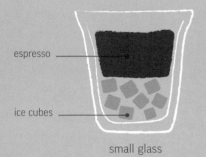

espresso

ice cubes

small glass

1 Place **3–4 ice cubes** and **a wedge of lemon** into the glass.

2 Using the technique on pp44–45, brew **two shots/ 50ml (1½fl oz) of espresso** over the ice.

SERVE IT UP Add **sugar syrup, if desired** (see pp162–63) to taste, and serve immediately.

ICE ESPRESSO

GEAR **ESPRESSO**   DAIRY **WITHOUT**   TEMP **COLD**   SERVES **1**

The quickest way to chill an espresso is to pour it over ice, but if you shake it with ice, you create an attractive foam. Experiment with different types of sugar – white, demerara, or muscovado – to provide contrasting flavours.

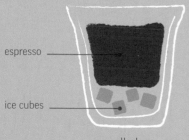

espresso

ice cubes

small glass

1 Using the technique on pp44–45, brew **two shots/50ml (1½fl oz) of espresso** into a small cup, and dissolve **sugar** into it, if desired.

2 Pour the espresso into a cocktail shaker filled with **ice cubes** and shake vigorously.

SERVE IT UP Fill the glass with a few **ice cubes**, strain the coffee over the top, and serve.

SPARKLING ESPRESSO

 GEAR **ESPRESSO**   DAIRY **WITHOUT**   TEMP **COLD**   SERVES **1**

Adding sparkling water to an espresso might seem an unusual practice, but the resulting effervescence is really quite refreshing. Beware that combining the two very abruptly might lead to an eruption of foam.

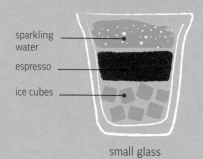

sparkling water

espresso

ice cubes

small glass

1 Place the glass in the freezer for an hour or so before you wish to serve.

2 Using the technique on pp44–45, brew **two shots/50ml (1½fl oz) of espresso** into a small jug. Fill the glass with **ice cubes** and pour the espresso over.

SERVE IT UP Gently top with **sparkling water**, taking care not to let the foam overflow, and serve.

SNOW WHITE

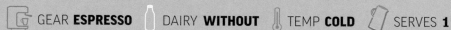 GEAR **ESPRESSO**   DAIRY **WITHOUT**   TEMP **COLD**   SERVES **1**

This chilled coffee combines the unusual flavours of strawberry and liquorice and is made with a lot of ice. The name of the recipe comes from the contrasting colours of red and black, which are reminiscent of Snow White's lips and hair.

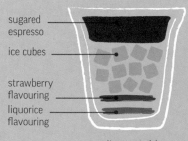

sugared espresso

ice cubes

strawberry flavouring

liquorice flavouring

medium tumbler

1 Using the technique on pp44–45, brew **two shots/50ml (1½fl oz)** of espresso into a jug. Dissolve **1 teaspoon white sugar** into it. Add the espresso and **ice cubes** to a cocktail shaker and shake vigorously.

2 Fill the tumbler with **1 tablespoon liquorice flavouring** and **1 tablespoon strawberry flavouring** and top with **ice cubes**.

3 Strain the espresso over. For a creamier flavour, add **50ml (1½fl oz) cold milk, if desired** before your pour the espresso over the top.

SERVE IT UP Serve with a spoon, to stir all the ingredients together.

SNOW WHITE You could try crushed
ice instead of ice cubes. It keeps the drink
cooler for longer – but will dilute quickly.

ESPRESSO COLA

GEAR **ESPRESSO**   DAIRY **WITHOUT**   TEMP **COLD**   SERVES **1**

A cold cola, flavoured with a shot of espresso, will keep you buzzing for a couple of hours. The two components can create a lot of froth when combined over ice, but keeping ingredients and glasses very cold will help.

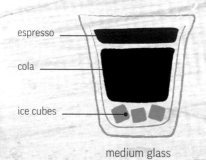

espresso

cola

ice cubes

medium glass

1 Using the technique on pp44–45, **brew one shot/25ml (1fl oz) of espresso** into a small jug and place it in the fridge until cold.

2 Add **ice cubes** to your glass and pour **150ml (5fl oz) cola** over the top. Allow the foam to subside, then gently pour over the cold espresso.

SERVE IT UP Sweeten to taste with **simple syrup** (see pp162–63), and serve.

RYAN DANDELION

GEAR **BREWER**   DAIRY **WITHOUT**   TEMP **COLD**   SERVES **4**

Roasted and ground dandelion root is a common alternative to coffee, as is chicory, barley, and sugar beet. Often used during times of rationing, these substitutes may not give you the caffeine hit, but can still be tasty and comforting.

dandelion root-brewed coffee

medium glass

1 Using the technique on p134, prepare cold-brewed coffee using a cold dripper. Brew **1 litre (1¾ pints) water**, **2 tablespoons medium-ground coffee**, **2 tablespoons roasted dandelion root**, and **2 tablespoons roasted sugar beet** or **chicory root** together.

3 Fill a cocktail shaker with **250ml (9fl oz) coffee** and **ice** per serving and shake well.

SERVE IT UP Pour into the glasses, garnish with **fresh dandelion flowers**, and serve immediately.

ICED CASCARA COFFEE

🍼 GEAR **BREWER**   🍶 DAIRY **WITHOUT**   🌡 TEMP **COLD**   🥤 SERVES **1**

Coffee usually comes from a roasted seed, but sometimes other parts of the coffee plant can be used to prepare traditional beverages like kuti, hoja, and qishr. Here, hibiscus-like cascara (dried coffee cherries) brighten up a cold brew.

coffee ice cubes and cascara ice cubes

cold-brewed coffee

medium glass

1 To prepare cascara ice cubes, make tea from **dried cascara**. Pour the infusion into an ice-cube tray and transfer to the freezer. Allow to freeze. Prepare coffee ice cubes the same way, by filling an ice-cube tray with **brewed coffee**.

2 Using the technique on p134, prepare **150ml (5fl oz) cold-brewed coffee** using a cold dripper.

3 Add the **cascara ice cubes** and **coffee ice cubes** to a cocktail shaker. Pour over the cold coffee, add **1 teaspoon dried cascara**, and shake.

SERVE IT UP **Pour into the glass, and serve immediately.**

ROOT OF ALL GOOD

🍼 GEAR **BREWER**   🍶 DAIRY **WITHOUT**   🌡 TEMP **COLD**   🥤 SERVES **1**

Root beer and coffee are especially pleasing when combined in a cold beverage. Instead of adding dairy, this recipe uses cream of coconut for texture and sweetness, which complements the root beer.

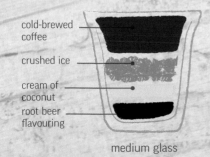

cold-brewed coffee

crushed ice

cream of coconut

root beer flavouring

medium glass

1 Using the technique on p134, prepare **150ml (5fl oz) cold-brewed coffee** using a cold dripper.

2 Add **50ml (1½fl oz) shop-bought root beer flavouring** and **50ml (1fl oz) cream of coconut** to the glass and mix well.

SERVE IT UP **Top with crushed ice**, pour the cold coffee over, and serve with a straw.

CREAM COFFEE POP

 GEAR **BREWER** DAIRY **WITHOUT** TEMP **COLD** SERVES **1**

Cream sodas come by many names, and in many versions and colours around the world. They can have different fruit flavours but usually taste of vanilla or sweetened milk.

ice-cold cream soda

ice-cold brewed coffee

coffee ice cubes

medium glass

1 Using the technique on p134, prepare **100ml (3½fl oz) ice-cold brewed coffee** using a cold dripper. Place the glass in the freezer for an hour or so.

2 Fill the frozen glass with **coffee ice cubes** (p189, iced cascara coffee, step 1) and pour over the coffee.

3 Slowly pour in **100ml (3½fl oz) ice-cold cream soda**. Take care not to let the foam overflow.

SERVE IT UP **Serve immediately.**

CARIBBEAN PUNCH

 GEAR **BREWER** DAIRY **WITHOUT** TEMP **COLD** SERVES **1**

Angostura bitters and the warm flavours of rum are brightened by lemon and sparkling water in this drink. To make rum ice cubes, add a little rum flavouring to water before pouring into an ice-cube tray and freezing.

sparkling soda water

rum–molasses mix

cold-brewed coffee

rum-flavoured ice cubes

medium glass

1 Using the technique on p134, prepare **150ml (5fl oz) cold-brewed coffee** using a cold dripper.

2 Fill the glass with **rum-flavoured ice cubes** and pour the cold coffee over the top.

3 In a jug, mix **2 teaspoons lemon juice, 5 drops angostura bitters, 25ml (1fl oz) rum flavouring**, and **1 tablespoon molasses**. Pour over the coffee and ice cubes.

SERVE IT UP Top up with **50ml (1½fl oz) sparkling soda water**, and serve.

COFFEE COLA FLOAT

GEAR **ESPRESSO**   DAIRY **SOYA ICE CREAM**   TEMP **COLD**   SERVES **1**

There are many good soya ice creams on the market, so if you cannot tolerate dairy, you can still experience the classic cola float. Be careful when you combine the cola and coffee, as it can get very foamy.

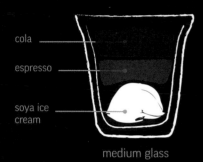

cola

espresso

soya ice cream

medium glass

1 Place **1 scoop soya ice cream** in the bottom of your serving glass.

2 Using the technique on pp44–45, brew **one shot/25ml (1fl oz) of espresso**. Pour it over the ice cream and carefully top up with **cola**.

SERVE IT UP Serve with a spoon.

ICE LATTE

GEAR **ESPRESSO**   DAIRY **MILK**   TEMP **COLD**   SERVES **1**

Refreshing on hot days, the ice latte can be shaken or stirred, sweetened or flavoured, and tailored to the strength you prefer. If you enjoy the more pronounced coffee taste of a cappuccino, use only half the milk in this recipe.

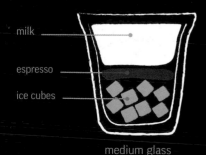

milk

espresso

ice cubes

medium glass

1 Fill half the glass with **ice cubes**. Using the technique on pp44–45, brew **1 shot/25ml (1fl oz) of espresso** into a small jug and pour it over the top.

SERVE IT UP Top up with **180ml (6fl oz) milk**, and sweeten to taste with **simple syrup** (see pp162–63).

ALTERNATIVELY Brew **1 shot/25ml (1fl oz) of espresso**, add it to **ice cubes** in a cocktail shaker, and shake well. Fill half the serving glass with **ice cubes** and add **180ml (6fl oz) milk** until the glass is three-quarters full. Strain the chilled espresso into the glass, and serve.

HAZELNUT ICE LATTE

GEAR **ESPRESSO** DAIRY **HAZELNUT MILK** TEMP **COLD** SERVES **1**

For a more complex dairy-free alternative, mix various nut and seed milks together and take the opportunity to play with textures as well. Sweetening with molasses instead of sugar adds another level of flavour.

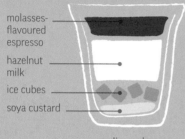

molasses-flavoured espresso

hazelnut milk

ice cubes

soya custard

medium glass

1 Using the technique on pp44–45, brew **two shots/50ml (1½fl oz) of espresso** into a small jug and dissolve **2 teaspoons molasses** into it. Add to a cocktail shaker filled with **ice cubes** and shake well.

2 Spoon **2 tablespoons soya custard** into the bottom of the glass and add a few **ice cubes**. Top up with **150ml (5fl oz) hazelnut milk**.

SERVE IT UP Strain the espresso over the top, and serve with a spoon.

RICE MILK ICE LATTE

GEAR **ESPRESSO** DAIRY **RICE MILK** TEMP **COLD** SERVES **1**

One of the more naturally sweet alternatives to cow's milk, rice milk does not froth well when steamed, but that makes it more suitable for iced coffees. Nut extracts go very well with rice milk, but experiment with berries as well.

praline espresso with rice milk

medium glass

1 Using the technique on pp44–45, brew **one shot/25ml (1fl oz) of espresso** into a small jug. Allow to cool.

2 Mix the espresso, **180ml (6fl oz) rice milk**, and **25ml (1fl oz) praline flavouring** in a cocktail shaker. Add some **coffee ice cubes** (see p189, iced cascara coffee, step 1) and shake vigorously.

SERVE IT UP Double-strain into the glass and serve immediately with a straw.

APRICOT STAR

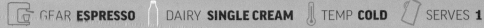

🖥 GEAR **ESPRESSO**   🍼 DAIRY **SINGLE CREAM**   🌡 TEMP **COLD**   📄 SERVES **1**

Combining tea and coffee works well with iced drinks, especially when enhanced with milk and other flavours. Use a single shot of espresso for a milder taste.

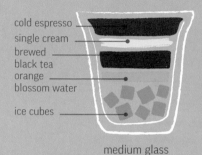

cold espresso
single cream
brewed
black tea
orange
blossom water

ice cubes

medium glass

1 Pour **150ml (5fl oz) boiling water** into a teapot. Steep **10g (¼oz) black tea leaves** with a **star anise**. Strain and chill.

2 Fill half the glass with **ice cubes**. Add **2 teaspoons orange blossom water** and **1 teaspoon apricot flavouring**. Pour the cold tea over the ice, and float **single cream** on top.

3 Using the technique on pp44–45, brew **two shots/50ml (1½fl oz) of espresso** into a small jug. Pour it into a cocktail shaker filled with **ice cubes**, and shake well until cold.

SERVE IT UP Strain the cold espresso into the glass and serve.

COCOMON

🖥 GEAR **ESPRESSO**   🍼 DAIRY **MILK**   🌡 TEMP **COLD**   📄 SERVES **1**

A small but sweet beverage, cocomon uses the delicious pairing of coconut and cinnamon to make you relish every last drop. You could replace the milk with single cream for a thicker texture.

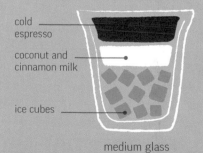

cold
espresso

coconut and
cinnamon milk

ice cubes

medium glass

1 Using the technique on pp44–45, brew **two shots/50ml (1½fl oz) of espresso** into a small jug, pour it over some **ice cubes** in a cocktail shaker, and shake well.

2 Fill half a glass with **ice cubes** and add **120ml (4fl oz) milk** until the glass is three-quarters full. Add **1 teaspoon each coconut and cinnamon flavourings**. Strain the chilled espresso into the glass.

SERVE IT UP Garnish with **coconut shavings**, sweeten to taste with **simple syrup** (see pp162–63), and serve.

ICE MOCHA Pure refreshment
on a summer's day, this drink is the
perfect post-barbecue pick-me-up.

ICE MOCHA

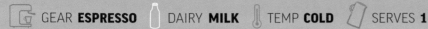 GEAR **ESPRESSO**   DAIRY **MILK**   TEMP **COLD**   SERVES **1**

A popular variation of the ice latte, the ice mocha requires chocolate sauce, which imparts a rich, sweet taste. If you would like the coffee flavour to come through more intensely, use less milk or reduce the amount of chocolate sauce.

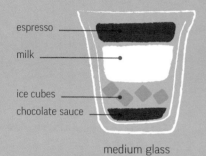

espresso

milk

ice cubes

chocolate sauce

medium glass

1 Pour **2 tablespoons light or dark chocolate sauce** (see pp162–63) into the glass. Fill with **ice cubes** and pour over **180ml (6fl oz) milk**.

2 Using the technique on pp44–45, brew **two shots/50ml (1½fl oz) of espresso** into a jug and pour it over the milk.

SERVE IT UP Serve immediately with a straw to help stir and dissolve the chocolate sauce.

BREATH OF FRESH AIR

 GEAR **ESPRESSO**   DAIRY **MILK**   TEMP **COLD**   SERVES **1**

Mint is a refreshing flavour pairing for coffee, and when rounded off with vanilla, it makes a beverage that is perfect for a summer's day. Choose a milk that is lower in fat for a more refined, elegant taste.

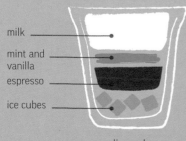

milk

mint and vanilla

espresso

ice cubes

medium glass

1 Using the technique on pp44–45, brew **two shots/50ml (1½fl oz) of espresso** into a jug. Fill about half the glass with **ice cubes** and carefully pour the espresso over it.

2 Add **1 teaspoon mint flavouring** and **5–6 drops vanilla essence**. Top up with **150ml (5fl oz) milk**.

SERVE IT UP Garnish with **mint leaves**, and serve with a spoon, to stir.

CA PHE SUA DA *Vietnamese iced coffee*

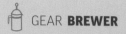 GEAR **BREWER**   DAIRY **CONDENSED MILK**   TEMP **COLD**   SERVES **1**

If you don't have a Vietnamese phin coffee dripper, use a French press (see p128) or a stove-top moka pot (see p133). Prepared in much the same way as the Ca phe sua nong (see p181), the iced version is more diluted, but still sweet and creamy.

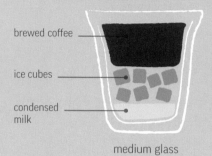

brewed coffee

ice cubes

condensed milk

medium glass

1 Pour **2 tablespoons condensed milk** into the bottom of the glass and fill with **ice cubes**.

2 Remove the filter from a phin (see p136) and pour **2 tablespoons medium-ground coffee** in. Shake to distribute the grounds and screw the filter back on.

3 Place the phin on top of the glass. Bring **120ml (4fl oz) water** to the boil and pour about a quarter of it over the filter. Using the phin, brew the coffee following the directions on p136.

SERVE IT UP Stir to dissolve the condensed milk, and serve.

CHERRY BERRY

 GEAR **BREWER**   DAIRY **MILK**   TEMP **COLD**   SERVES **1**

Many coffee-producing regions, such as Kenya and some regions of Colombia, produce coffee beans that feature fruit-like flavour characteristics. These often lend themselves very well to being prepared using the cold-brewing technique.

whipped cream

double-strength cold-brewed coffee

milk
ice cubes
cranberry flavouring
cherry flavouring

tall glass

1 Using the technique on p134, brew **200ml (7fl oz) cold coffee double-strength** over **ice cubes**.

2 Pour **25ml (1fl oz) cherry flavouring** and **1 tablespoon cranberry flavouring** into the bottom of the glass and fill it half full with **ice cubes**. Carefully pour over **50ml (1½fl oz) milk** and then the coffee.

SERVE IT UP Top with **1 tablespoon whipped cream**, garnish with a **fresh cherry**, and serve with a spoon.

PISTACHIO BUTTER

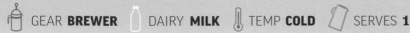

GEAR **BREWER**   DAIRY **MILK**   TEMP **COLD**   SERVES **1**

The taste of peanuts in coffee is sometimes associated with low quality, but it is not the case for all varieties. Try a nutty coffee for this – the strawberry and pistachio flavourings evoke the flavour combination of peanut butter and jelly.

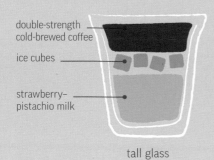

double-strength
cold-brewed coffee

ice cubes

strawberry–
pistachio milk

tall glass

1 Using the technique on p134, brew **50ml (1½fl oz) double-strength coffee** over **ice cubes**.

2 Add **ice cubes**, **120ml (4fl oz) milk**, **1 tablespoon pistachio flavouring**, and **1 tablespoon strawberry flavouring** to a cocktail shaker and shake well.

3 Pour into the glass and add some more **ice cubes**. Carefully pour the coffee over the top.

SERVE IT UP Garnish with a **fresh strawberry** on the rim of the glass, and serve.

ICE MAPLE LATTE

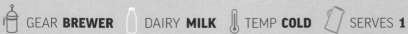

GEAR **BREWER**   DAIRY **MILK**   TEMP **COLD**   SERVES **1**

For a simple twist on an iced café au lait, mix in maple syrup. This not only adds sweetness, but also highlights how the melting coffee ice cubes steadily intensify the coffee flavour of this beverage.

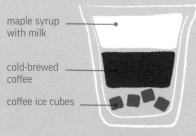

maple syrup
with milk

cold-brewed
coffee

coffee ice cubes

medium glass

1 Using the technique on p134, prepare **120ml (4fl oz) cold-brewed coffee** using a cold dripper.

2 Add **coffee ice cubes** (see iced cascara coffee, step 1, p189) to your glass. Pour over the coffee and **120ml (4fl oz) milk**.

SERVE IT UP Drizzle with **maple syrup to taste** over the floating ice cubes, and serve with a stirrer.

MILK AND HONEY Frozen milk cubes or coffee cubes prevent the coffee drink from diluting too much.

MILK AND HONEY

 GEAR **BREWER**   DAIRY **MILK**   🌡 TEMP **COLD**   SERVES **1**

Honey is a flavoursome natural sweetener and works well In both hot and cold drinks. In this recipe, you can add it to the coffee before it is chilled, or stir in just before serving. To make milk cubes, simply freeze milk in an ice-cube tray.

double-strength
cold-brewed
coffee

milk

heather
honey blend
milk ice cubes

tall glass

1 Using the technique on p134, brew **100ml (3½fl oz) cold-brewed coffee** double-strength over **ice cubes**.

2 Place **3–4 frozen milk cubes** into the glass and add **½ teaspoon vanilla extract**, **1 tablespoon heather honey**, and **¼ teaspoon ground cinnamon**.

SERVE IT UP Pour **100ml (3½fl oz) milk** followed by the coffee into the glass, and serve with a stirring spoon.

BLENDED ICE COFFEE

☕ GEAR **ESPRESSO**   🍼 DAIRY **MILK**   🌡 TEMP **COLD**   SERVES **1**

Like a coffee milkshake, this creamy, smooth concoction can be enjoyed on its own or flavoured with any number of ingredients. If you prefer a lighter texture, replace the cream with regular milk or use low-fat milk.

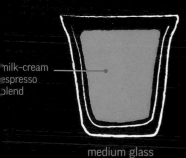

milk-cream
espresso
blend

medium glass

1 Using the technique on pp44–45, brew **one shot/25ml (1fl oz) of espresso** into a small jug.

2 Pour the espresso, **5–6 ice cubes**, **30ml (1fl oz) cream**, and **150ml (5fl oz) milk** into a blender, and mix until smooth.

SERVE IT UP Sweeten to taste with **simple syrup** (see pp162–63), and serve in the glass with a straw.

FRAPPÉ MOCHA

GEAR **ESPRESSO**　DAIRY **MILK**　TEMP **COLD**　SERVES **1**

For a twist on blended ice coffee, add some chocolate sauce and increase the amount of espresso to balance out the flavours. Try a milk chocolate sauce for a milder taste, or go for a white chocolate sauce.

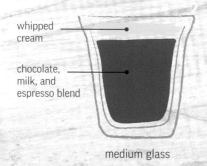

whipped cream

chocolate, milk, and espresso blend

medium glass

1 Using the technique on pp44–45, brew **two shots/50ml (1½fl oz) of espresso** into a small jug.

2 Pour the **espresso**, **180ml (6fl oz) milk**, **2 tablespoons chocolate sauce**, and **5–6 ice cubes** into a blender, and mix until smooth. Sweeten to taste with **simple syrup** (see pp162–63).

SERVE IT UP Pour into the glass, top with **1 tablespoon whipped cream**, and serve with a straw.

CHOC–MINT FRAPPÉ

GEAR **ESPRESSO**　DAIRY **MILK**　TEMP **COLD**　SERVES **1**

Like an After Eight dipped in coffee, this cool drink is a great post-dinner treat: rich and smooth with the beautiful pairing of mint and chocolate underpinned by the espresso. Sweeten to taste, and enjoy with a chocolate mint.

chocolate, milk, mint, and espresso blend

medium glass

1 Using the technique on pp44–45, brew **two shots/50ml (1½fl oz) of espresso** into a small jug.

2 Pour the **espresso**, **5–6 ice cubes**, **180ml (6fl oz) milk**, **25ml (1fl oz) mint flavouring**, and **2 tablespoons chocolate sauce** into a blender, and mix until smooth. Sweeten to taste with **simple syrup** (see pp162–63).

SERVE IT UP Pour into the glass, garnish with **chocolate shavings** and **mint leaves**, and serve. For a pretty serving vessel, try a coupette glass.

HAZELNUT FRAPPÉ

🖳 GEAR **ESPRESSO**   🍼 DAIRY **WITHOUT**   🌡 TEMP **COLD**   🥤 SERVES **1**

Hazelnut milk is a dairy-free option that matches well with coffee and is easy to make at home. With the addition of vanilla, the flavours blend together perfectly.

hazelnut milk, vanilla, and espresso blend

medium glass

1 Using the technique on pp44–45, brew **two shots/50ml (1½fl oz) of espresso** into a small jug.

2 Pour the **espresso**, **200ml (7fl oz) hazelnut milk**, **5–6 ice cubes**, and **1 teaspoon vanilla sugar** into a blender, and mix until smooth.

SERVE IT UP Pour into the glass, and serve with a straw.

HORCHATA FRAPPÉ

🖳 GEAR **ESPRESSO**   🍼 DAIRY **WITHOUT**   🌡 TEMP **COLD**   🥤 SERVES **4**

Horchata is a Latin American drink made from almonds, sesame seeds, tigernuts, or rice. Vanilla and cinnamon are common flavourings. You can make your own or buy it ready-made.

rice milk, horchata, and brewed coffee blend

small wine glass

1 Using the technique on p131, brew **100ml (3½fl oz) strong coffee** using an AeroPress.

2 Pour the **coffee**, **2 tablespoons horchata powder**, **100ml (3½fl oz) rice milk**, **seeds from 2 vanilla pods**, **½ teaspoon ground cinnamon**, and **10–15 ice cubes** into a blender, and mix until smooth.

SERVE IT UP Add **simple syrup to taste** (see pp162–63), garnish with **vanilla pods** or **cinnamon sticks**, and serve.

COFFEE LASSI

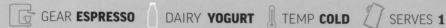 GEAR **ESPRESSO** DAIRY **YOGURT** TEMP **COLD** SERVES **1**

Yogurt works well as an alternative to milk, imparting a fresh taste and adding texture to a blended beverage on par with cream or ice cream. A scoop of frozen yogurt can be substituted for the plain yogurt in this recipe.

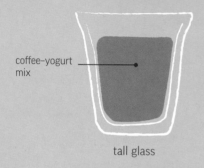

coffee-yogurt mix

tall glass

1 Using the technique on pp44–45, brew **two shots/50ml (1½fl oz) of espresso** into a small jug.

2 Place **5–6 ice cubes** in a blender, and pour the espresso over the top. Allow to cool.

3 Add **150ml (5fl oz) yogurt**, **1 teaspoon vanilla flavouring**, **1 teaspoon honey**, and **2 tablespoons chocolate sauce** to the blender. Mix till smooth.

SERVE IT UP Sweeten to taste with additional honey, and serve in the glass with a straw.

LOVE LIQUORICE

 GEAR **ESPRESSO** DAIRY **MILK** TEMP **COLD** SERVES **1**

If you like the unique flavour of liquorice, you'll enjoy this drink. You can find blendable liquorice in powder, syrup, or sauce form. Experiment with the intensity and try a salty liquorice for some extra bite.

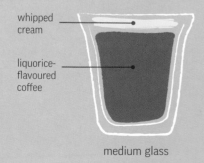

whipped cream

liquorice-flavoured coffee

medium glass

1 Using the technique on pp44–45, brew **two shots/50ml (1½fl oz) of espresso** into a small jug.

2 Pour the espresso, **180ml (6fl oz) milk**, **1 teaspoon liquorice powder**, and **5–6 ice cubes** into a blender and mix until smooth.

3 Sweeten to taste with **simple syrup** (see pp162–63), and pour into the glass.

SERVE IT UP Top with **1 tablespoon whipped cream**, sprinkle with some more **liquorice powder**, garnish with a **star anise**, and serve with a straw.

ICE CREAM RUM RAISIN

GEAR **ESPRESSO**   DAIRY **MILK**   TEMP **COLD**   SERVES **1**

Rum and raisin is a classic flavour pairing most commonly enjoyed in ice cream. The two also work really well with coffee, as both flavours are often used to describe the flavour profile of naturally processed beans.

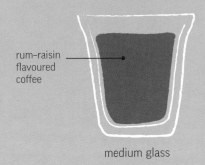

rum-raisin flavoured coffee

medium glass

1 Using the technique on pp44–45, brew **two shots/50ml (1½fl oz) of espresso** into a small jug.

2 Pour the espresso, **120ml (4fl oz) milk**, **25ml (1fl oz) rum-raisin flavouring**, and **1 scoop vanilla ice cream** into a blender. Mix until smooth.

3 Sweeten to taste with **simple syrup** (see pp162–63), and pour into the glass.

SERVE IT UP Top with **whipped cream, if desired**, and serve with a straw.

VOLUPTUOUS VANILLA

GEAR **ESPRESSO**   DAIRY **MILK**   TEMP **COLD**   SERVES **1**

Making a blended beverage with condensed milk adds a certain voluptuous texture that will make it feel like you're drinking liquid silk. If you prefer it less sweet, you could try evaporated milk or single cream instead.

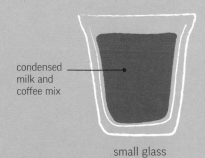

condensed milk and coffee mix

small glass

1 Using the technique on pp44–45, brew **one shot/25ml (1fl oz) of espresso** into a small jug.

2 Pour the espresso, **100ml (3½fl oz) milk**, **2 tablespoons condensed milk**, **1 teaspoon vanilla extract**, and **5–6 ice cubes** into a blender and mix until smooth.

SERVE IT UP Pour into the glass, and serve immediately.

MALTED MIX

GEAR ESPRESSO   **DAIRY MILK**   **TEMP COLD**   SERVES **1**

Nondiastatic malt powder is used in drinks as a sweetening agent. Use it here for sweet flavour and a thick, comforting texture. You could use malted milk powder instead – chocolate malt works, too.

milk, malt, and
espresso blend

beer mug

1 Using the technique on pp44–45, brew **two shots/50ml (1½fl oz) of espresso** in a small jug.

2 Pour the **espresso**, **1 small scoop chocolate ice cream**, **5–6 ice cubes**, **150ml (5fl oz) milk**, and **2 tablespoons malt powder** into a blender, and mix until smooth.

SERVE IT UP Pour into the mug, and serve immediately with **malted milk biscuits** on the side.

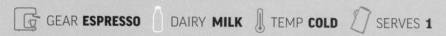

MOCHA BANANA

GEAR ESPRESSO   **DAIRY MILK**   **TEMP COLD**   SERVES **1**

Fresh banana is difficult to blend with coffee, but when frozen and blended with ice, milk, vanilla, and chocolate, it works beautifully. Like a coffee-flavoured smoothie, this drink is invigorating, filling, and refreshing.

milk, vanilla,
banana,
chocolate, and
espresso blend

medium tumbler

1 Using the technique on pp44–45, brew **two shots/50ml (1½fl oz) of espresso** in a small jug.

2 Pour the **espresso**, **150ml (5fl oz) milk**, **½ teaspoon vanilla extract**, **5–6 ice cubes**, **½ ripe frozen banana**, **1 tablespoon chocolate sauce**, and **2 teaspoons sugar** into a blender, and mix until smooth.

SERVE IT UP Pour into the tumbler, decorate with a vanilla pod and slice of banana, and serve.

ESTONIAN MOCHA

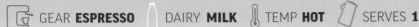

GEAR **ESPRESSO**   DAIRY **MILK**   TEMP **HOT**   SERVES **1**

Vana Tallinn is a rum-based liqueur with hints of citrus, cinnamon, and vanilla, all frequently noted flavours in high-quality coffees. With the addition of some chocolate sauce, this becomes a caffè mocha with a kick.

espresso

steamed milk

Vana Tallinn

chocolate sauce

cosmopolitan glass

1 Pour **1 tablespoon chocolate sauce** and **30ml (1fl oz) Vana Tallinn** into the glass, mixing well.

2 Steam **120ml (4fl oz) milk** in a pitcher to about 60-65°C (140-150°F) or until the pitcher is just too hot to touch (see pp48-51). Pour it carefully into the glass.

3 Using the technique on pp44-45, brew **two shots/50ml (1½fl oz) of espresso** into a small jug.

SERVE IT UP Pour the espresso into the glass, and serve.

RECOMMENDED BEANS Coffees with hints of citrus, cinnamon, and vanilla.

CORRETTO ALLA GRAPPA

GEAR **ESPRESSO**   DAIRY **WITHOUT**   TEMP **HOT**   SERVES **1**

An espresso corretto is a shot of espresso "corrected" with a shot of spirit or liquor, usually Grappa, but sometimes Sambuca, Brandy, or Cognac. The shot is usually added before serving, but you can also serve it on the side.

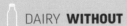

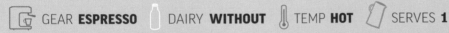

Grappa

espresso

demitasse cup

1 Using the technique on pp44-45, brew **one shot/25ml (1fl oz) of espresso** into your cup.

2 Pour **25ml (1fl oz) Grappa**, or any spirit of your choice, over the top of your espresso.

SERVE IT UP Serve immediately.

RON DULCE

GEAR **ESPRESSO**   DAIRY **WHIPPED CREAM**   TEMP **HOT**   SERVES **1**

Caramel is a flavour that goes seriously well with coffee. This recipe embraces that taste combination with creamy dulce de leche, added coffee flavour from the sweet Kahlua, and a warming sensation from the rum.

whipped cream
espresso
Kahlua
rum
dulce de leche

medium glass

1 Pour **1 tablespoon dulce de leche** into the glass. Pour over **25ml (1fl oz) rum** and **1 tablespoon Kahlua**.

2 Using the technique on pp44–45, brew **two shots/50ml (1½fl oz) of espresso** into a small jug and pour it over the alcohol.

3 Whisk **25ml (1fl oz) whipped cream** until thickened but not stiff.

SERVE IT UP Layer the cream on top, pouring it in off the back of a spoon, and serve.

PANDA ESPRESSO

GEAR **ESPRESSO**   DAIRY **WITHOUT**   TEMP **HOT**   SERVES **1**

Mint and liquorice is a classic combination that pairs well with coffee. Using a green Crème de Menthe here can make for an interesting visual experience, but if you don't like the idea of a green drink, try a clear Crème de Menthe instead.

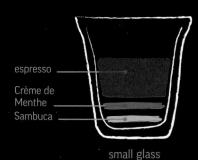

espresso
Crème de Menthe
Sambuca

small glass

1 Pour **1 tablespoon Sambuca** and **1 tablespoon Crème de Menthe** into the glass.

2 Using the technique on pp44–45, brew **two shots/50ml (1½fl oz) of espresso** into a small jug and pour it carefully into the glass.

SERVE IT UP Garnish with a **fresh mint leaf**, and serve.

PANDA ESPRESSO If you prefer not to down your drinks in one, give this espresso shot a little stir before sipping.

RUSTY SHERIDANS

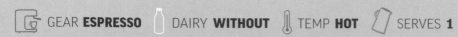

GEAR **ESPRESSO**   DAIRY **WITHOUT**   TEMP **HOT**   SERVES **1**

Inspired by the Rusty Nail, the most famous Drambuie cocktail, this recipe leads with whisky, but adds Sheridans for sweetness and to make the coffee flavour more pronounced. For a brighter note, let the lemon twist infuse in the espresso.

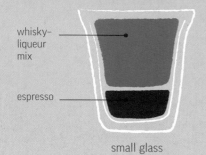

whisky–
liqueur
mix

espresso

small glass

1 Using the technique on pp44–45, brew **1 shot/25ml (1fl oz) of espresso** into the glass.

2 Mix **25ml (1fl oz) Drambuie**, **25ml (1fl oz) Sheridans**, and **50ml (1½fl oz) whiskey** in a jug and pour the mixture carefully into the glass, allowing the crema of the espresso to sit on the rising surface as you pour.

SERVE IT UP Garnish with **a lemon twist**, and serve.

IRISH COFFEE

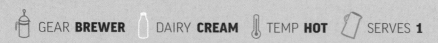

GEAR **BREWER**   DAIRY **CREAM**   TEMP **HOT**   SERVES **1**

Joe Sheridan created the Irish Coffee in 1942, and it has since become the most famous coffee-based drink in the world. It mixes coffee (strong as a friendly hand) and whiskey (smooth as the wit of the land) with sugar and cream.

whipped
cream

whiskey

brewed
coffee

Irish coffee glass

1 Using the technique on p129, brew **120ml (4fl oz) strong coffee** in a pour-over filter.

2 Pour the coffee and **2 teaspoons brown sugar** into the glass, and stir until the sugar dissolves.

3 Add **30ml (1fl oz) Irish whiskey** and stir. Lightly whip **30ml (1fl oz) cream** until it thickens but doesn't become stiff.

SERVE IT UP Float the cream on top of the coffee by pouring it gently off the back of a spoon, and serve.

ACROSS THE EQUATOR

 GEAR **BREWER**   DAIRY **DOUBLE CREAM**   TEMP **HOT**   SERVES **1**

The Norwegian Linie Aquavit, a herb-infused spirit, spends months maturing at sea, on board ships that cross the equator twice on a round trip to Australia. Norwegians love their coffee as well – here these two drinks mix in a unique way.

double cream

Linie Aquavit

brewed coffee

large mug

1 Brew **150ml (5fl oz) coffee** using a French press (p128), AeroPress (p131), or brewer of your choice. Pour it into the mug.

2 Add **1 teaspoon sugar**, and stir until dissolved. Add **30ml (1fl oz) Linie Aquavit** and float **50ml (1½fl oz) double cream** on top.

SERVE IT UP Garnish with **a fennel sprig**, and serve.

ORCHARD RUM

 GEAR **BREWER**   DAIRY **WITHOUT**   TEMP **HOT**   SERVES **1**

Apples and coffee might not seem like an obvious pairing, but they complement each other very well. If you can't find Applejack, other apple-based liqueurs such as Calvados or Pommeau make perfect replacements.

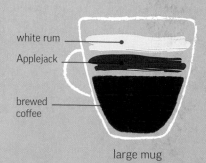

white rum

Applejack

brewed coffee

large mug

1 Brew **240ml (8fl oz) coffee** using a French press (p128), AeroPress (p131), or brewer of your choice.

2 Mix the coffee in the mug with **30ml (1fl oz) Applejack** and **30ml (1fl oz) white rum**.

SERVE IT UP Sweeten to taste with **molasses**, and serve.

RECOMMENDED BEANS Apple-based spirits highlight the soft fruit notes of many good-quality Central American coffees.

COGNAC BRULOT

GEAR **BREWER**   DAIRY **WITHOUT**   TEMP **HOT**   SERVES **1**

This variation of the classic New Orleans Caffè Brulot uses either Cognac or brandy as the spirit. Caffè Brulot was invented by Jules Alciatore at Antoine's Restaurant during the Prohibition – the citrus and spice were a clever way to conceal alcohol.

brewed coffee

spiced Cognac

snifter glass

1 Pour **30ml (1fl oz) Cognac** into the glass and keep it warm using a brandy warmer. Add **1 teaspoon brown sugar**, **1 cinnamon stick**, **1 clove**, **1 lemon twist**, and **1 orange twist**.

2 Brew **about 150ml (5fl oz) coffee** using a French press (see p128), AeroPress (see p131), or brewer of your choice. Pour it into the glass. If the angle of the snifter means the coffee will overflow, take it off the brandy warmer stand before filling.

SERVE IT UP Stir with the cinnamon stick until the sugar is dissolved and the ingredients have infused, and serve.

AVERIN CLOUD

GEAR **BREWER**   DAIRY **CREAM**   TEMP **HOT**   SERVES **1**

The averin is an amber-coloured berry most commonly known as cloudberry or bakeapple. Inspired by the Norwegian dessert "Multekrem", which combines averin jam and whipped cream, this recipe adds grape vodka for a twist.

whipped cream

vodka

Lakka

brewed coffee

medium glass

1 Brew **180ml (6fl oz) coffee** using a French press (see p128), AeroPress (see p131), or brewer of your choice.

2 Pour the **coffee** into the glass and pour **30ml (1fl oz) Lakka** and **30ml (1fl oz) Cîroc**, or **other fruit-based vodka**, over the top.

SERVE IT UP Whip **100ml (3½fl oz) cream** with a **dash of Lakka**, float a layer on top of the drink, and serve.

CREAM VERMOUTH

🍼 GEAR **BREWER**　🥛 DAIRY **ICE CREAM**　🌡 TEMP **HOT**　🥤 SERVES **1**

Flavoured with herbs, Vermouth contributes complexity to this cocktail, which uses chocolate ice cream for sweetness. You can stir the ice cream to melt it, or serve with a spoon.

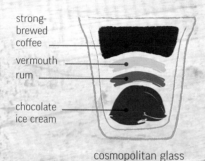

strong-brewed coffee

vermouth

rum

chocolate ice cream

cosmopolitan glass

1. Place **1 scoop chocolate ice cream** at the bottom of the glass, and pour **30ml (1fl oz) rum** and **30ml (1fl oz) vermouth** over the top.

2. Brew **180ml (6fl oz) strong coffee** using a French press (see p128), AeroPress (see p131), or brewer of your choice.

SERVE IT UP Pour it gently into the glass, sweeten to taste with **brown sugar**, and serve.

ESPRESSO MARTINI

📠 GEAR **ESPRESSO**　🥛 DAIRY **WITHOUT**　🌡 TEMP **COLD**　🥤 SERVES **1**

This is an elegant drink that can be enjoyed with or without the added sweetness of a chocolate liqueur such as Crème de Cacao. If you don't want to use the Crème de Cacao, double your quantity of Kahlua.

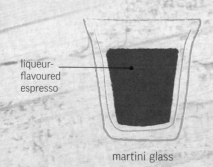

liqueur-flavoured espresso

martini glass

1. Using the technique on pp44–45, brew **two shots/50ml (1½fl oz) of espresso**. Let it cool slightly.

2. Combine the **coffee** with **1 tablespoon Crème de Cacao**, **1 tablespoon Kahlua**, and **50ml (1½fl oz) vodka** in a cocktail shaker. Add **ice cubes** and shake well. If you combine the espresso and alcohol first, the liquid will be cooler and the ice cubes won't melt as much.

SERVE IT UP Double strain into the glass, garnish the foam with **3 coffee beans**, and serve.

GIN CHAMBORD

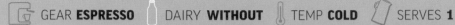

GEAR **ESPRESSO**   DAIRY **WITHOUT**   TEMP **COLD**   SERVES **1**

Coffee is easily paired with most fresh berries. This dairy-free cocktail with gin and grapefruit juice perfectly complements the ingredients of the Chambord. Some simple syrup counteracts the acidity of the fresh berries.

boozey
raspberry-
espresso mix

coupette glass

1 Using the technique on pp44–45, brew **two shots/50ml (1½fl oz) of espresso** into a small jug. Let it cool slightly.

2 Crush **5 raspberries** with **25ml (1fl oz) Chambord** and then mix in a cocktail shaker with **20ml (½fl oz) simple syrup** (see pp162–63), **25ml (1fl oz) gin**, and **1 tablespoon grapefruit juice**. Add **ice cubes** to the shaker, and pour the espresso over.

SERVE IT UP Shake well and strain into the glass. Garnish with **a raspberry** on the rim of the glass, and serve.

CHARTREUSE HARD SHAKE

GEAR **ESPRESSO**   DAIRY **MILK**   TEMP **COLD**   SERVES **1**

When added to ice cream, the herbal flavours of Chartreuse liqueur mellow, and the combination creates a great alternative to dessert. Reduce the quantity of milk if you prefer a thicker texture. For contrast, decorate with coffee beans.

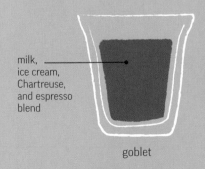

milk,
ice cream,
Chartreuse,
and espresso
blend

goblet

1 Using the technique on pp44–45, brew **two shots/50ml (1½fl oz) of espresso** into a small jug.

2 Pour the espresso, **150ml (5fl oz) milk** and **50ml (1½fl oz) Chartreuse liqueur** into a blender, add **1 scoop ice cream**, and mix until smooth.

SERVE IT UP Pour into the goblet, and serve.

RECOMMENDED BEANS Chartreuse and ice cream complement many washed Ethiopian coffees.

GRAND CHOCOLATE

GEAR **ESPRESSO**   DAIRY **WITHOUT**   TEMP **COLD**   SERVES **1**

Chocolate and orange is a classic flavour combination, and combined with Bourbon and espresso, the complexity of aromas makes this drink a firm after-dinner favourite. You could try it served hot – simply take out the ice cubes.

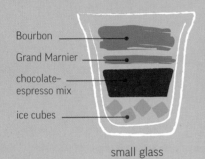

Bourbon
Grand Marnier
chocolate-espresso mix
ice cubes

small glass

1 Using the technique on pp44–45, brew **two shots/50ml (1½fl oz) of espresso** into a small jug, and stir in **1 teaspoon chocolate sauce** (see pp162–63) until it melts.

2 Place **4–5 ice cubes** in the glass and pour the chocolate–espresso mix over. Stir until the espresso cools. Add **1 tablespoon Grand Marnier** and **50ml (1½fl oz) Bourbon**.

SERVE IT UP Garnish with **an orange twist**, and serve.

COLD KIRSCH

GEAR **ESPRESSO**   DAIRY **WITHOUT**   TEMP **COLD**   SERVES **1**

Evocative of a liquid Black Forest Gâteau, you could serve this drink with dark chocolate truffles or a rich chocolate ice cream. Cool the espresso completely before adding the egg white, and double strain to achieve the creamy texture.

Cognac-brandy espresso mix

goblet

1 Place **ice cubes** in a cocktail shaker. Using the technique on pp44–45, brew **two shots/50ml (1½fl oz) of espresso** over the top, allowing to cool.

2 Pour **25ml (1fl oz) Cognac**, **25ml (1fl oz) cherry brandy**, and **2 teaspoons egg white** into the shaker, and shake well. Double strain into the goblet.

SERVE IT UP Sweeten to taste with **simple syrup** (see pp162–63), and serve.

PORT CASSIS Place your glass in the
freezer for an hour or so before serving,
to help to keep the coffee cool.

PORT CASSIS

GEAR **ESPRESSO**   DAIRY **WITHOUT**   TEMP **COLD**   SERVES **1**

Fortified wines match beautifully with coffee, especially if you brew
an espresso from a bean that shares the same fruit characteristics.
Crème de Cassis adds a layer of sweetness to round it all off.

Port

espresso

Crème de
Cassis

ice cubes

snifter glass

1 Place **4–5 ice cubes** in the snifter glass, and pour in **25ml (1fl oz) Crème de Cassis**.

2 Using the technique on pp44–45, brew **one shot/25ml (1fl oz) of espresso** into the snifter, and stir to cool the coffee. Gently pour in **75ml (2½fl oz) Port**.

SERVE IT UP Garnish with **a blackberry**, and serve.

RECOMMENDED BEANS The fruity and wine-like notes in a good Kenyan coffee will complement the berries and Port.

REGAN DISARONNO

GEAR **BREWER**   DAIRY **WITHOUT**   TEMP **COLD**   SERVES **1**

Disaronno (considered an Amaretto), is a liqueur flavoured with apricot oil,
herbs, and fruits. The almond and apricot flavourings complement the liqueur,
while the mocha sauce makes this drink taste of chocolate-covered almonds.

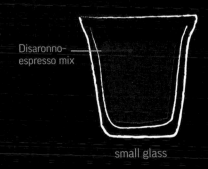

Disaronno-
espresso mix

small glass

1 Brew **100ml (3½fl oz) coffee** using a French press (see p128), AeroPress (see p131), or brewer of your choice. Allow to cool.

2 Pour the cooled coffee with **25ml (1fl oz) Disaronno**, **1 tablespoon mocha sauce**, **ice cubes**, and **5–6 drops each almond and apricot flavourings** into a cocktail shaker, and shake well. Double-strain into the glass.

SERVE IT UP Scatter some **chocolate shavings** over, and serve.

GREEN FAIRY JUNIPER

 GEAR **BREWER**   DAIRY **WITHOUT**   TEMP **COLD**   SERVES **1**

Absinthe, with its liquorice flavour, goes really well with the juniper in gin and makes this a unique drink. If you can't find Absinthe easily, Pernod is another flavoursome – and often less potent – replacement.

Absinthe–gin coffee cocktail

margarita glass

1 Brew **75ml (2½fl oz) cold coffee** using a French press (see p128), AeroPress (see p131), or brewer of your choice. Allow to cool.

2 Pour the coffee, **25ml (1fl oz) gin**, **25ml (1fl oz) Absinthe**, **3 teaspoons simple syrup** (see pp162–63), and **ice cubes** into a cocktail shaker, and shake well.

SERVE IT UP Double-strain into the glass, float a **star anise** on top, and serve.

RECOMMENDED BEANS Beans with herbal overtones, such as a classic Ethiopian light roast, can add a layer of complexity and refreshment.

RUMMY CAROLANS

 GEAR **BREWER**   DAIRY **WITHOUT**   TEMP **COLD**   SERVES **1**

Sometimes sweet and warming is what you want, even from an iced cocktail. This combination of rum and Carolans with the boost of coffee flavour from the Tia Maria gives you just that – refreshment and comfort.

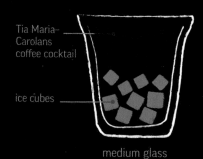

Tia Maria–Carolans coffee cocktail

ice cubes

medium glass

1 Fill a saucer with a little **rum** and another with **sugar**. Wet the rim of the glass in the rum, then dip it into the sugar.

2 Using a French press (see p128), AeroPress (see p131), or brewer of your choice, brew **75ml (2½fl oz) double-strength coffee** over **ice cubes**.

3 Pour the coffee, **1 tablespoon Tia Maria**, **1 tablespoon Carolans**, **25ml (1fl oz) rum**, and **sugar to taste** into a cocktail shaker, and shake.

SERVE IT UP Fill the glass with **ice cubes**, double-strain the drink over the top, and serve.

MEXICAN LIMELIGHT

GEAR **BREWER** DAIRY **WITHOUT** TEMP **COLD** SERVES **1**

Mexico grows coffee, makes tequila, and produces agave nectar. Mix the three with lime, and you have a beverage that has a lower glycaemic index than a drink sweetened with sugar. Choose a dark agave for a more caramelized taste.

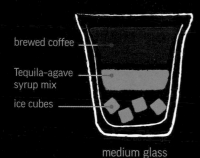

brewed coffee

Tequila-agave
syrup mix

ice cubes

medium glass

1 Place **4–5 ice cubes** in the glass. Brew **100ml (3½fl oz) coffee** using a French press (see p128), AeroPress (see p131), or brewer of your choice. Allow to cool.

2 In another glass, dissolve **1 tablespoon light agave nectar** in **50ml (1½fl oz) tequila** and pour it over the ice cubes, followed by the cold coffee.

SERVE IT UP Run a **slice of lime** around the edge of the glass, hang it on the rim, and serve.

HAZEL KRUPNIK

GEAR **BREWER** DAIRY **WITHOUT** TEMP **COLD** SERVES **1**

Honey is a great alternative to sugar, and in this recipe, Krupnik (a sweet alcoholic drink popular in Poland and Lithuania) adds the honey flavour while lemon vodka keeps the drink from becoming too sweet and heavy.

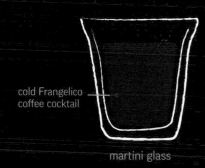

cold Frangelico
coffee cocktail

martini glass

1 Using a French press (see p128), AeroPress (see p131), or brewer of your choice, brew **50ml (1½fl oz) double-strength coffee** over **ice cubes**.

2 Pour the coffee, **1 tablespoon Frangelico**, **1 tablespoon Krupnik**, **25ml (1fl oz) lemon vodka**, and **ice cubes** into a cocktail shaker and shake well.

SERVE IT UP Double-strain into the glass, garnish with a **vanilla pod**, and serve.

RECOMMENDED BEANS The hazelnut and vanilla notes in Frangelico go beautifully with the sweet, nutty Brazilian coffees (see pp92–93).

GLOSSARY

ARABICA One of two commercially grown species of coffee *(see also Robusta)*. Arabica is the higher quality species of the two.

BENEFICIOS A Spanish word for a processing mill (either wet or dry).

BURRS Discs in grinders that crush coffee beans into particle sizes for brewing or espresso.

CAFFEINE A chemical found in coffee that contributes to feelings of alertness.

CHAFF The thin layer of skin that covers a roasted coffee bean.

COFFEE CHERRY The fruit of the coffee tree. It is surrounded by a skin, and contains mucilage, parchment, and, usually, two coffee seeds.

COLD-BREWED COFFEE Coffee that is prepared with a dripper tower and cold water, or a hot brew that is allowed to cool.

COMMODITY MARKET The coffee trade market in New York, Brazil, London, Singapore, and Tokyo.

CREMA The layer of foam that forms on top of an espresso.

CULTIVAR A cultivated variety *(see also Variety)* intentionally bred for consumption.

CUPPING The practice of tasting and evaluating coffees.

DE-GASSING The practice of leaving beans to release gases created during the roasting process.

DEMITASSE A "half cup" – typically referring to a 90ml (3oz) espresso cup with a handle.

DOSE A measure of coffee intended for brewing with water.

EXTRACTION A process that occurs during brewing, when coffee solubles dissolve into water.

GREEN BEANS Raw, unroasted coffee beans.

HYBRID A cross between two species of coffee.

MUCILAGE The sticky, sweet fruit meat or pulp surrounding the parchment-covered coffee seeds inside a coffee cherry.

NATURAL PROCESS The practice of processing coffee cherries by leaving them out to dry in the sun.

PEABERRIES Single (as opposed to double) round seeds that may be found inside coffee cherries.

POTATO DEFECT The raw potato smell and taste attributed to coffee beans affected by a certain bacteria.

PULPED NATURAL PROCESS The practice of processing coffee cherries by removing skin but leaving mucilage intact before they are left out to dry.

ROBUSTA One of two commercially grown species of coffee *(see also Arabica)*. Robusta is the lower quality species of the two.

SOGESTAL The managing body of Burundian washing stations, akin to Cooperative Societies in Kenya.

TAMPING The practice of compacting ground coffee in the filter basket of an espresso machine.

TRACEABILITY The assertable origin, source, information, and backstory of a coffee.

VARIETY A taxonomy class describing members of a species – such as Arabica – that have identifiable differences.

WASHED PROCESS The practice of processing coffee cherries by removing skin and mucilage with soaks and rinses, before leaving parchment-covered beans out to dry in the sun.

INDEX

Page numbers in *italic* indicate step-by-step techniques and those in **bold** indicate coffee or flavouring recipes.

AUTHOR

Anette Moldvaer is the co-founder of Square Mile Coffee Roasters, a multi-award winning coffee roasting company based in London, England. Square Mile source, buy, import, and roast coffees to sell to consumers and businesses. Anette began her career as a barista in her native Norway in 1999, and now visits coffee producers all year round, sourcing the best coffees from around the world.

Anette judges international industry competitions, such as the World Barista Championships, the Cup of Excellence, and the Good Food Awards, and has led coffee workshops all over Europe, the United States, Latin America, and Africa. She roasted the winning espresso at the World Barista Championship in 2007, 2008, and 2009, and won the World Cup Tasters Championship in 2007.

ACKNOWLEDGMENTS

Anette would like to thank:
Martha, Kathryn, DK, Tom, and Signe; Krysty, Nicky, Bill, SQM, San Remo, and La Marzocco; Emma, Aaron, Giancarlo, Luis, Lyse, Piero, Sunalini, Gabriela, Sonja, Lucemy, Mie, Cory, Christina, Francisco, Anne, Bernard, Veronica, Orietta, and Rachel; Stephen, Chris, and Santiago; Ryan, Marta, Chris, Mathilde, Tony, Joanne, Christian, Bea, Grant, Dave, Trine, and Morten; Margarita, Vibeke, Karna, Stein, and my coffee family and friends.

DK would like to thank:
Photography William Reavell
Art direction Nicola Collings
Prop styling Wei Tang
Additional photography and latte art Krysty Prasolik
Proofreading Claire Cross
Indexing Vanessa Bird
Editorial assistance Charis Bhagianathan
Design assistance Mandy Earey, Anjan Dey, and Katherine Raj
Creative technical support Tom Morse and Adam Brackenbury

Thanks also to Augusto Melendrez at San Remo. Key Fact statistics featured on pp56–123 are based on the 2008–2012 ICO figures, apart from those on pp85, 88, 116, 117, and 120.
Picture credits: p17 top Bethany Dawn; p26 Claire Cordier; pp68, 115, 121 Anette Moldvaer.

A NOTE ON THE MAPS
Coffee bean icons show the location of notable coffee-producing regions on the maps on pp56–123. Green shading indicates coffee production over a larger area – either within political boundaries or over approximate climate-driven geographical areas.

A NOTE ON THE RECIPES
For best results, refer to these recommended volumes. **Cups** demitasse – 90ml/3fl oz; small – 120ml/4fl oz; medium – 180ml/6fl oz; large – 250ml/9$\frac{1}{2}$fl oz. **Mugs** small – 200ml/7fl oz; medium – 250ml/9$\frac{1}{2}$fl oz; large – 300ml/10$\frac{1}{2}$fl oz. **Glasses** small – 180ml/6fl oz; medium – 300ml/10$\frac{1}{2}$fl oz; tall – 350ml/12fl oz.